BERLIN
Travel Guide

The Ultimate Travel Book To Unveiling Berlin Hidden Gems

Brian Mathew

Copyright © by **Brian Matthew**

All rights reserved. No part of this publication may be reproduced, distributed, or transmitted in any form or by any means, including photocopying, recording, or other electronic or mechanical methods, without the prior written permission of the publisher, except in the case of brief quotations embodied in critical reviews and certain other noncommercial uses permitted by copyright law.

Table of Contents

Brief History 7
Geography 10
Tourists Must Know Things Before Visiting 13
Best Touring Apps and websites 17
Top Activities 20
    Hiking 20
        Top Hiking Spots 21
        Essential Tips 21
        Guided Hiking Tours 22
    Watersports 24
        Safety Considerations 27
    Inline Skating 28
    Rock Climbing 31
Dialects and Language 34
Weather 37
Getting Here 40
    By Air 40
    By Train 40
    By Car 41
Top Attractions 43
    Brandenburg Gate 43
    Reichstag Building 46

Berlin Wall Memorial ... 49
Checkpoint Charlie ... 52
Museumsinsel ... 55
East Side Gallery ... 58
Charlottenburg Palace ... 61
Memorial to the Murdered Jews of Europe ... 63
Tiergarten ... 66
Gendarmenmarkt ... 69
Fernsehturm ... 71
DDR Museum ... 74
Berlin Philharmonic ... 77
Berliner Unterwelten ... 80
Topography of Terror ... 83
Hackesche Höfe ... 86
Nikolaiviertel ... 89
Berlinische Galerie ... 91
Tempelhofer Feld ... 94
Mauerpark ... 97
Treptower Park ... 100
Berlin Dungeon ... 103
Clärchens Ballhaus ... 106
Berliner Dom Museum ... 109
Stasi Museum ... 112

- Hamburger Bahnhof 115
- Friedrichshain Volkspark 118
- Top Cuisine to Try Out 121
  - Currywurst 121
  - Döner Kebab 124
  - Eisbein 126
  - Schnitzel 128
  - Kartoffelsalat 130
  - Labskaus 132
  - Buletten 134
  - Spätzle 136
  - Flammkuchen 138
  - Sauerbraten 140
- Best Time To Visit 143
- Traveling Itinerary 146
- Visiting On a Budget 149
- Getting Around 152
- Shopping for Souvenirs 155
  - Best Places for Souvenir Shopping 155
  - Types of Souvenirs 156
  - Shopping Tips for an Enjoyable Experience 157
- Tour Package Options 159
- Tourist Safety Tips 162

Festival and Events.. 165

Brief History

Berlin, the capital of Germany, possesses a rich and compelling past that has molded its character as one of the most active and prominent cities in Europe. From its humble beginnings as a medieval trading village to its partition during the Cold War and subsequent reunification, Berlin's journey is a fascinating tale of endurance, evolution, and success.

The story of Berlin begins around the 13th century when it was created as a small town along the River Spree. The city's strategic location made it a key trading hub, leading to its fast growth and ultimate elevation to the rank of a major mercantile town. In 1701, Berlin became the capital of the Kingdom of Prussia under the authority of Frederick I, which marked the beginning of its ascent as a political powerhouse in the region.

During the 19th century, Berlin witnessed enormous breakthroughs in culture, arts, and sciences. This era, dubbed as the "Golden Twenties," saw the city becoming a hub of intellectual and creative triumphs, with figures such as Albert Einstein and Marlene Dietrich calling it home. However, this golden period was short-lived as the establishment of the Nazi dictatorship in the 1930s plunged the city into the darkness of the Third Reich.

One of the worst chapters in Berlin's history is certainly the reign of Adolf Hitler and the Nazi Party. In 1933, Hitler came to power, and Berlin became the capital of Nazi Germany. The city suffered immense repression, persecution, and the systematic slaughter of millions of Jews and other minority groups during the Holocaust. World War II left considerable damage on Berlin, with the city undergoing unrelenting Allied bombardment and the Battle of Berlin in 1945. The defeat of Nazi Germany led to the split of Berlin into East and West, mirroring the division of the entire country.

The split of Berlin came to symbolize the greater geopolitical divide of the Cold War. West Berlin, a democratic enclave, was surrounded by communist East Germany and functioned as a symbol of resistance against Soviet encroachment. The Berlin Wall, completed in 1961 by East Germany, physically separated the two halves of the city, leading to sad tales of families ripped apart and daring escape attempts. The Wall stood as a terrible reminder of the ideological strife until 1989 when the peaceful revolution led to its fall, signaling the end of the Cold War and the eventual reunification of Germany.

The reunification of Berlin on October 3, 1990, began a new chapter in the city's history. The fall of the Wall paved the ground for the city's restoration and reunification. As East and West Berlin joined, the city went on a journey of renewal and reinvention, becoming a symbol of unity and optimism for the globe.

In the years following reunification, Berlin had a spectacular recovery, establishing itself as a thriving cultural center. The city's dynamic cultural scene, avant-garde architecture, and cutting-edge technology have attracted people from all over the world. Berlin's rich history is tangible when visitors explore prominent sights such as the Brandenburg Gate, the Reichstag Building, and the remnants of the Berlin Wall.

Today, Berlin is not just the political and economic center of Germany but also a beacon of creativity, variety, and tolerance. The scars of its stormy past are maintained in its memorials and museums, serving as heartbreaking reminders of the city's resilience and the need of sustaining peace and democracy.

Conclusion

Berlin's history is a rich tapestry of successes and tragedies. From its modest origins as a trading settlement to its reputation as a worldwide city, the history of Berlin illustrates the resilience and energy of its people. Understanding the city's past is crucial to comprehending its present and the journey it has followed to become a symbol of optimism, unity, and progress in the 21st century.

Geography

Berlin is a fascinating metropolis with a rich history and a diversified geographical location that has played a vital influence in determining its growth. Situated in northeastern Germany, Berlin is placed at the center of Europe, making it a significant political, cultural, and economic center. The city's landscape contains a range of features, including its position in the North European Plain, the River Spree, forests, parks, and urban sprawl.

Location and Topography
Berlin is situated on the banks of the River Spree, a navigable waterway that has historically enabled trade and transit. The city lies in the North European Plain, a huge lowland that runs across numerous European countries. This flat terrain influenced Berlin's expansion and allowed it to grow outward rather than upward, resulting in a wide cityscape with several neighborhoods and districts.

Districts and Boroughs
Berlin is divided into 12 administrative districts, each encompassing multiple neighborhoods. Some of the prominent districts include Mitte, the central district housing major landmarks and government buildings; Friedrichshain-Kreuzberg, known for its vibrant nightlife and cultural diversity; Charlottenburg-Wilmersdorf, an affluent area with historical sites; and Neukölln, a rapidly changing district with a diverse population.

River Spree and Waterways
The River Spree not only adds to Berlin's aesthetic splendor but also serves a practical role in the city's transportation

system. It connects numerous districts and boroughs through a network of canals and waterways, providing an alternative form of mobility for both tourists and inhabitants. The Spree also offers leisure opportunities, with boat cruises and riverfront activities being popular among locals and visitors alike.

Parks and Green Spaces

Despite being a crowded city, Berlin features various parks and natural spaces, adding to its reputation as a green metropolis. The most notable among these is the Tiergarten, a huge park in the center of the city that provides a lush respite for urban inhabitants. Additionally, the Grunewald forest, located in the southwest, offers chances for hiking and outdoor activities. These green areas add to Berlin's great quality of life and serve as crucial recreational sites for its inhabitants.

Urban Sprawl and Infrastructure

Berlin's flat topography has allowed for substantial urban sprawl, with the city steadily expanding over the years. The growth of residential neighborhoods, commercial zones, and industrial districts has led to the establishment of a well-connected transportation infrastructure, comprising an extensive network of buses, trams, trains, and subways. The Berlin Hauptbahnhof, one of Europe's largest railway stations, operates as a crucial transit hub connecting the city to different national and international destinations.

Historical Significance

Berlin's terrain has also played a vital role in molding its history, particularly throughout the 20th century. During World War II, the city's strategic location made it a popular target for bombing attacks, leading to substantial destruction. The subsequent separation of Berlin by the Berlin Wall (1961-1989) altered the city's environment and established major geographical and cultural contrasts between East and West Berlin.

Contemporary Urban Challenges

In recent years, Berlin has encountered several issues relating to its terrain and urban development. The city's status as an affordable and exciting destination has attracted a considerable inflow of residents, putting pressure on housing and infrastructure. Additionally, climate change poses a hazard, with rising temperatures and shifting precipitation patterns needing adaptation techniques to sustain the city's green spaces and water resources.

Conclusion

Berlin's terrain has played a major influence in shaping its metropolitan landscape and historical significance. The River Spree, flat geography, green spaces, and transportation networks have all contributed to the city's development as a dynamic and bustling metropolis. As Berlin continues to evolve, it must confront contemporary urban difficulties while conserving the particular geographical elements that have made it an amazing European capital.

Tourists Must Know Things Before Visiting

Before visiting Berlin, it's vital for travelers to educate themselves on many facets of the city to ensure a seamless and enjoyable experience. As the capital of Germany, Berlin provides a fascinating blend of history, culture, and modernity that attracts millions of visitors each year. To make the most of your trip, below are crucial facts for tourists:

History and Culture
The city is lined with historical landmarks like the Brandenburg Gate, Berlin Wall ruins, and the Reichstag Building. To properly grasp Berlin's past, try visiting museums like the Topography of Terror, the Jewish Museum, and the DDR Museum. It's also vital to grasp the significance of the Berlin Wall, which divided the city from 1961 to 1989 and shaped its contemporary character.

Currency and Payment
Germany uses the Euro (€) as its official currency so is its capital city. Despite the widespread acceptance of credit and debit cards, it's a good idea to have some cash on hand for smaller transactions and places that might not accept cards.

Safety and Etiquette
Berlin is generally a secure city for travelers, but it's always wise to apply common sense. Be careful of pickpockets in crowded locations and follow local customs and etiquette, such as greeting people with a handshake and saying "danke" (thank you) after receiving a service.

Tipping
Tipping is common in Berlin, however, it's not as significant as in some other nations. A 5-10% tip at restaurants and cafés is welcomed, and you can round up the cost for taxi drivers and other services.

Opening Hours
Shops in Berlin normally open from Monday to Saturday, with some larger establishments shutting earlier on Saturdays. Sundays and public holidays frequently feature restricted shopping alternatives, with many places closed.

Health and Travel Insurance
Healthcare in Germany is good but can be pricey for foreigners. Consider purchasing travel insurance that covers medical crises, trip cancellations, and other unanticipated catastrophes.

Accommodation Options
Berlin offers a wide selection of housing options to suit all budgets and interests. From luxurious hotels to cozy hostels and vacation rentals, you'll find something that meets your needs. It's important to book your accommodation in advance, especially during peak tourist seasons.

Nightlife and Entertainment
Berlin's nightlife is famed, featuring a diversity of bars, clubs, and live music venues. The city's electronic music culture is highly recognized. Be sure to visit districts like Kreuzberg, Friedrichshain, and Prenzlauer Berg, where you'll discover a bustling environment and numerous entertainment alternatives.

Parks and Gardens

Berlin is a green city with many parks and gardens where you may relax and unwind. Tiergarten, the city's major park, is great for leisurely strolls or picnics. Additionally, explore the stunning gardens of Sanssouci Palace in nearby Potsdam for a great day excursion.

Wi-Fi and Connectivity

Stay connected throughout your visit with the city's free Wi-Fi offered in many public spaces like parks, squares, and transportation hubs. If you need constant internet connectivity, try getting a local SIM card with data or using a portable Wi-Fi hotspot.

Environmental Consciousness

Berlin takes pride in its eco-friendliness and sustainability projects. Recycling is an integral aspect of the city's culture, therefore be sure to follow the appropriate waste separation standards during your visit.

Photography and Privacy

While Berlin is a lovely city, always be cautious of people's privacy and the restrictions regulating photography. Avoid taking images of someone without their agreement, especially in sensitive or private areas.

Accessibility

Berlin is moderately accessible for tourists with impairments, with many public transport stations equipped with elevators and ramps. Additionally, several museums and attractions offer customized services for guests with mobility issues.

Emergency Contacts

In case of emergency, remember to contact 112 for police, fire, and medical aid. The city has a good healthcare system, and hospitals can be located throughout Berlin.

By familiarizing yourself with these vital aspects, you'll be well-prepared to discover Berlin's rich history, culture, and dynamic atmosphere. Remember to be respectful, open-minded, and adventurous as you embark on your tour through this lively metropolis.

Best Touring Apps and websites

To enhance their stay and make the most of their time in the city, travelers can employ different touring applications and websites that provide important information, navigation aid, and insights into Berlin's hidden gems. Here are some of the greatest touring apps and websites that offer a complete experience for travelers visiting Berlin.

VisitBerlin.de (*www.visitberlin.de/en*): As the official tourism website for Berlin, VisitBerlin.de is a great starting point for any tourist. This comprehensive website offers a lot of information about destinations, events, lodgings, and public transportation alternatives. Tourists can plan their itineraries, discover lesser-known landmarks, and explore Berlin's many districts with this user-friendly website.

Visit A City (*www.visitacity.com/*): Visit A City is a popular software that provides customizable itineraries depending on travelers' preferences and available time. In Berlin, users can access pre-planned trips to iconic monuments like the Brandenburg Gate, the Reichstag, and the Berlin Wall. The program also offers insights into local eateries, retail districts, and nightlife spots, allowing travelers to experience Berlin like a local.

TripAdvisor (*www.tripadvisor.com/*): TripAdvisor remains a go-to site for travelers globally. In Berlin, the app's large database of reviews and ratings lets travelers make informed selections about where to eat, stay, and visit. It also includes user-generated content on off-the-beaten-path destinations, making it an ideal resource for individuals seeking unique experiences.

BVG FahrInfo Plus (*iOS & Android*): For navigating Berlin's large public transit network, BVG FahrInfo Plus is an important app. Tourists can get real-time information regarding buses, trams, and trains, ensuring efficient transport between attractions. The app also offers a route planner, ticket purchase choices, and service updates, making it an invaluable tool for travelers visiting the city.

GetYourGuide (*www.getyourguide.com/*): GetYourGuide is a famous platform that offers a wide choice of guided tours and activities in Berlin. From walking tours to bike rides, and historical excursions to gastronomic activities, travelers can find various options to fit their interests. The platform also allows users to reserve skip-the-line tickets for major sights, saving crucial time during their visit.

Spotted by Locals (*www.spottedbylocals.com/berlin/*): For an authentic Berlin experience, Spotted by Locals is the go-to app. It delivers exclusive advice and recommendations from residents who know the city inside out. From the best street food locations to hidden bars, this app helps travelers discover Berlin beyond the conventional tourist traps.

Komoot (*https://www.komoot.com/*): Komoot is a perfect app for outdoor enthusiasts wishing to explore Berlin's natural parks and surrounding nature paths. It includes thorough hiking and bike itineraries, complete with maps, elevation profiles, and sites of interest. Tourists may escape the urban buzz and immerse themselves in Berlin's gorgeous landscapes by utilizing this app.

Conclusion

Berlin is a city with a vast assortment of attractions and experiences to offer, and these touring apps and websites serve as vital tools for any tourist's investigation. Whether visitors seek historical insights, quirky excursions, or efficient navigation, these resources provide a thorough and unforgettable experience in one of Europe's most engaging towns. So, take your smartphone, download these applications, and get ready to start on a thrilling adventure through the heart of Berlin.

Top Activities

Berlin offers an abundance of physical outdoor activities for travelers to enjoy. From historical buildings to extensive parks and rivers, the city presents a broad choice of attractions for nature lovers, adventure enthusiasts, and those wanting an active holiday. Here are some of the top physical outdoor activities in Berlin

Hiking

Berlin is recognized for its rich history, cultural treasures, and vibrant city life. However, few people are aware of the wonderful hiking options that await just beyond the city limits. Surrounding Berlin, you'll find a broad range of natural landscapes, lush forests, stunning lakes, and lovely trails suited for hikers of all levels. Here are the greatest hiking sites, necessary information, and what you can expect during your hiking excursion in Berlin.

Top Hiking Spots

Grunewald Forest: Grunewald is a big forested area located in the western suburbs of Berlin. It offers a large network of trails amidst tall trees, modest hills, and magnificent lakes like the Teufelssee. The Teufelsberg, a man-made hill erected from the ruins of World War II, offers amazing panoramic views over the city and the surrounding area.

Wannsee and Pfaueninsel: Combine culture and nature with a trek around Wannsee Lake and a visit to the Pfaueninsel (Peacock Island). The island is a UNESCO World Heritage site and is home to peacocks and several other animals. The trails around the lake offer calm vistas and are suitable for a relaxed day trip.

Schönower Heide: Located northeast of Berlin, this natural reserve boasts wide heathland, woodlands, and a serene ambiance. The trails here are great for nature enthusiasts and birdwatchers.

Müggelsee: Berlin's largest lake, Müggelsee, has various hiking trails around its shoreline. You may trek through the Köpenick Forest, enjoy lake vistas, and even take a boat tour if you'd want to experience the lake from a different perspective.

Essential Tips

Seasonal Considerations: Berlin undergoes diverse seasons, so plan your hike accordingly. Spring and autumn bring nice weather, while summers can be sweltering. Winters are freezing, and trekking on icy trails requires adequate attire.

Trail Difficulty: Most hiking paths near Berlin are suitable for beginners and families. However, some paths could have steeper sections or uneven terrain, so choose trails that meet your fitness level and tastes.

Weather Preparedness: Berlin's weather can be unpredictable, so always check the forecast before heading out. Bring necessities like water, snacks, a map, sunscreen, and adequate clothing, including rain gear, if necessary.

Respect Nature and Wildlife: Berlin's surrounding surroundings are precious ecosystems. Respect wildlife, respect authorized trails, and keep from polluting.

Transportation: S-Bahn trains, regional trains, and buses connect the city with several hiking destinations. For Grunewald and Wannsee, take the S-Bahn to Grunewald or Wannsee station. To reach Schönower Heide, take the S2 to Bernau and transfer to a local bus.

Guided Hiking Tours

If you prefer a guided experience or want to learn more about the area's history and wildlife, consider joining a guided hiking tour. Many local tour companies provide scheduled hikes to various places, providing a skilled guide to augment your experience.

Safety Precautions
While hiking around Berlin is generally safe, mishaps can happen. Always inform someone about your planned path,

especially if you're hiking alone. Carry a fully charged phone and a first aid kit with you. In case of an emergency, phone 112—the European emergency number.

Watersports

Many tourists are typically shocked to realize that this bustling metropolis also provides a wealth of fascinating water sports activities. With numerous lakes, rivers, and canals snaking through the city, water sports fans will find plenty of possibilities to participate in exhilarating aquatic experiences. Here are the many water sports accessible in Berlin, highlighting popular places, safety issues, and the optimum times to indulge in these activities.

Sailing and Windsurfing

Berlin boasts several lovely lakes that are suitable for sailing and windsurfing. The most popular of them is Lake Wannsee, located in the southwestern section of the city. Sailing clubs and rental facilities may be located along its borders, offering travelers the ability to explore the tranquil seas and enjoy spectacular views of the surrounding countryside.

For those new to sailing or windsurfing, there are various schools that offer courses and equipment rentals, making it accessible to novices and specialists alike. It's advisable to check the weather forecast and inquire about the current wind conditions before stepping out for a safe and enjoyable trip.

Kayaking and Canoeing
Berlin's large network of rivers and canals gives a wonderful chance for kayaking and canoeing enthusiasts. The River Spree, in particular, offers a superb urban paddling experience, allowing travelers to glide by historic monuments such as the Berlin Cathedral, Museum Island, and the Reichstag building. Additionally, the Landwehr Canal, with its tree-lined banks and lovely bridges, provides a calm and tranquil setting for a leisurely paddle.

Numerous rental firms and guided trips are available, catering to different skill levels and tastes. Paddling along Berlin's waterways not only provides a unique perspective of the city but also allows travelers to interact with nature despite the urban bustle.

Stand-up Paddleboarding (SUP)
Stand-up paddleboarding has become more popular in Berlin, giving a fun and interesting way to explore the city's water bodies. SUP allows travelers to stand on a huge, solid board and use a paddle to move through the water. It's a superb full-body workout and a perfect alternative for families or parties searching for a shared water sport activity.

Lake Tegel and Schlachtensee are two popular sites for stand-up paddleboarding, providing tranquil waters and attractive surroundings. Many rental stores provide essential equipment, and beginners can rapidly acquire the basics with the help of teachers.

Wakeboarding
For adrenaline enthusiasts wanting an action-packed water sport, wakeboarding is a top choice. Wakeboarders are pulled across the water's surface by a cable system, allowing them to do stunts and jumps. The Wakeboard Park in Berlin offers an exciting wakeboarding experience, complete with ramps, jumps, and obstacles.

Whether you're a seasoned wakeboarder or a beginner, the park provides an entertaining environment for all abilities. Safety clothing and equipment are available for hire, assuring a safe and fun journey.

Swimming and Diving
Berlin's lakes are not just for sports fans; they also give fantastic chances for swimming and diving. During the warm summer months, various lakes, such as Wannsee and Schlachtensee, become popular swimming places for locals and tourists alike. Many lakes have dedicated swimming areas with lifeguards on duty, ensuring a safe environment for swimmers.

For those interested in diving, various lakes offer diving areas with unique underwater landscapes, including buried structures and rich aquatic life. However, keep in mind that diving may require suitable certification and safety procedures.

Safety Considerations

While partaking in water activities in Berlin, travelers should consider safety at all times, here are some safety considerations:

Weather and Water Conditions: Check weather forecasts and water conditions before indulging in any water activity. Avoid water activities during storms, severe winds, or rapidly changing weather.

Personal Floatation Devices (PFDs): Always use a PFD, especially if you're not a strong swimmer.

Stay Hydrated: Bring plenty of water to stay hydrated, especially on hot summer days.

Know Your Limits: Be conscious of your skill level and physical capabilities. Don't attempt advanced water sports without sufficient training and experience.

Follow Rules and Guidelines: Respect the local rules and guidelines of each water sports area to ensure a safe and fun experience for everyone.

Inline Skating

Inline skating in Berlin is an exhilarating and popular activity that allows travelers to discover the city in a unique and energetic way. With its smooth roads, picturesque routes, and bustling urban environments, Berlin offers a perfect location for inline skating enthusiasts of all abilities.

One of the biggest attractions for inline skaters in Berlin is the enormous network of well-maintained pathways and trails. The city boasts a wide network of bike lanes and pedestrian routes, which are great for inline skating. The pathways are generally flat and smooth, making them excellent for beginners to acquire a grip on the sport while still providing a comfortable experience for expert skaters.

One of the most iconic inline skating routes in Berlin is the Berliner Mauerweg or Berlin Wall Trail. This pathway follows the former path of the Berlin Wall, allowing skaters a unique opportunity to discover the city's history while gliding through diverse districts and sites. The path is around 160 kilometers long, but skaters can choose specific areas to explore based on their interests and fitness levels.

For those who want a more relaxed experience, Tiergarten Park is a good choice. Located in the center of the city, this wide green oasis provides a tranquil and scenic atmosphere for inline skaters. Skating around the tree-lined paths, through lovely lakes, and antique statues is a delightful way to spend a sunny afternoon in Berlin.

Inline skating tours are very popular in the city. These guided excursions allow guests the chance to explore Berlin's biggest landmarks on skates while learning about the city's history and culture from professional guides. Skating tours generally cover monuments such as the Brandenburg Gate, Checkpoint Charlie, and Museum Island, providing a unique and energetic viewpoint on the city's attractions.

For those seeking a more adrenaline-pumping experience, the Tempelhofer Feld is a must-visit site. This abandoned airport has been turned into a big public area, and its wide-open runways provide a perfect site for speed skating and more difficult stunts. The Tempelhofer Feld also holds skateboarding competitions, making it a magnet for action sports fans in Berlin.

Safety is of essential concern while inline skating in Berlin. Tourists should use appropriate protective gear, including helmets, knee pads, and wrist guards, to limit the chance of injuries. It's crucial to be careful of pedestrians and cyclists on shared pathways and to respect traffic regulations when crossing roadways.

Inline skating is a year-round activity in Berlin, with many locals and tourists enjoying the sport throughout the warmer months. However, it's vital to verify weather conditions before stepping out, as rainy or slippery conditions can make skating risky.

Rock Climbing

While Berlin may not boast natural cliffs and mountains, it has established an innovative urban rock climbing scene that has garnered popularity among locals and visitors alike.

Rock climbing in Berlin has progressed from its humble origins in the early 20th century to a popular adventure activity. Initially, climbers explored opportunities in the adjacent sandstone rock formations of Saxon Switzerland and the Elbe Sandstone Mountains. However, as the popularity of the sport expanded, Berliners began looking for closer and more accessible climbing possibilities within the city borders.

Today, Berlin features a choice of sophisticated indoor climbing gyms that cater to climbers of all skill levels. These gyms offer a secure and supervised environment for beginners to learn the ropes and seasoned climbers to refine their techniques. Some popular climbing gyms are Magic

Mountain, Bright Site, and Ostbloc. These facilities are equipped with state-of-the-art climbing walls, bouldering areas, and competent instructors, making them the perfect places for tourists to experience the thrill of climbing.

While the city may not have natural rock formations ideal for traditional outdoor climbing, Berlin's inventive climbers have transformed its concrete jungle into an urban climbing paradise. The renowned Teufelsberg, an artificial hill built on the wreckage of World War II, today serves as a popular outdoor bouldering destination with routes appropriate for all levels. Additionally, the Mauerpark climbing wall, located near the famous flea market, offers another fascinating outdoor climbing experience for adventurers.

As with any adventure sport, safety is paramount in rock climbing. Berlin's climbing gyms maintain tight safety measures, ensuring climbers are equipped with adequate gear and receive proper training before taking on the walls. Climbing outdoors needs additional caution, and tourists are urged to climb with experienced locals who are familiar with the area and can provide essential guidance on climbing ethics, respecting the environment, and reducing influence on the urban surroundings.

Berlin's climbing community is a tight-knit and inclusive group of enthusiasts from varied origins. Visitors will find abundant options to connect with fellow climbers through local climbing clubs, online forums, and meetup groups. Participating in climbing sessions and events with locals not only enriches the whole experience but also provides essential insights into Berlin's climbing culture and the city's distinctive areas for bouldering and climbing.

Conclusion

Berlin's vibrant outdoor scene appeals to all inclinations and fitness levels, making it an ideal destination for travelers seeking physical activities within a rich cultural setting. Whether cycling through history, kayaking on the River Spree, or picnicking in a calm park, Berlin promises an unforgettable and energetic experience for every visitor. So, pack your kit and be ready to embrace the fun that Berlin's outdoors has to offer.

Dialects and Language

Berlin is a melting pot of civilizations, and its language landscape reflects this diversity. Berlin's past has played a key part in developing its dialects and languages, making it a fascinating destination for language enthusiasts and curious tourists alike.

The official language spoken in Berlin, as in the rest of Germany, is Standard German. Standard German, also known as Hochdeutsch (High German), serves as the lingua franca and is utilized in education, media, government, and business relations. Tourists will discover that most individuals in Berlin can communicate in Standard German, making it quite straightforward for travelers to get around and engage with locals.

However, Berlin's linguistic tapestry goes beyond Standard German, and various unique dialects may be heard around the city. The most noteworthy of these is Berlinerisch, which is the local dialect spoken by native Berliners. Berlinerisch is a Low German dialect, which means it is part of the broader group of dialects spoken in Northern Germany.

Berlinerisch has its distinct accent, vocabulary, and even grammar compared to Standard German. The most noticeable feature of this dialect is the loss of the last "-e" in words and the substitution of some vowels and consonants. For example, "gute" (good) in Standard German becomes "gut" in Berlinerisch. While the dialect is more usually heard among older generations, it still retains a special place in the hearts of Berliners and is retained in local dialogues and folklore.

As Berlin has become a multicultural city due to immigration and globalization, many additional languages are spoken by distinct populations throughout the city. Turkish, for instance, is commonly spoken due to the considerable Turkish minority in Berlin. Arabic is also prevalent, especially due to the influx of refugees and immigrants from Arabic-speaking nations.

English is another regularly spoken language in Berlin, notably among the younger population and those working in the tourism, hospitality, and technological sectors. Tourists from English-speaking countries will find it quite easy to communicate with locals, particularly in famous tourist sites.

Berlin's history is also profoundly connected with the legacy of the Soviet Union, as it was divided into East and West Berlin during the Cold War. Consequently, Russian is still spoken by certain elderly people, and certain Russian cultural features have left an indelible impact on the city's legacy.

Overall, Berlin's linguistic diversity offers tourists a unique opportunity to explore diverse cultures and languages. Respect for the various languages spoken in the city is vital, as it symbolizes the cosmopolitan fabric of Berlin and the openness of its inhabitants towards different communities.

As a tourist, it's necessary to be mindful of the cultural sensitivities surrounding language use. While many locals can speak English or are accustomed to talking with non-German speakers, making an effort to acquire a few simple phrases in German can go a long way in bridging the language gap and demonstrating respect for the local culture.

Conclusion

Berlin's linguistic environment is an intriguing reflection of its rich history and varied makeup. From the native Berlinerisch dialect to the great diversity of languages spoken by distinct communities, travelers can immerse themselves in a completely diversified linguistic experience. Embracing this language diversity can lead to meaningful connections with locals and a deeper respect for Berlin's distinctive cultural heritage.

Weather

Berlin features a temperate seasonal climate that is distinguished by various fluctuations throughout the year. Understanding the weather patterns in Berlin is vital for travelers preparing to visit the city since it can drastically affect their trip experience and activities.

Spring (March through May)
Spring in Berlin symbolizes the end of the chilly winter months and the onset of milder, more pleasant weather. March can still be chilly, with temperatures ranging from 2°C to 10°C (36°F to 50°F), but as the season continues, the days become longer and warmer. April sees average temperatures between 5°C and 14°C (41°F and 57°F), and by May, the weather starts to seem truly spring-like, with temperatures ranging from 9°C to 19°C (48°F to 66°F).

During the spring months, tourists may watch the city's parks and gardens springing to life with brilliant blossoms and greenery. It's a wonderful time for outdoor activities such as seeing historical buildings, motorcycling along the Spree River, or admiring the beautiful cherry blossoms at the Kirschblütenallee.

Summer (June to August)
Summer in Berlin is warm and relatively sunny, making it the main tourist season. Average temperatures range from 13°C to 23°C (55°F to 73°F) in June and can go up to 17°C to 24°C (63°F to 75°F) in July and August. Occasionally, temperatures can soar considerably higher, especially during heatwaves.

This season is great for outdoor events, music festivals, and dining in open-air cafes. The city's lakes, such as Wannsee and Müggelsee, became popular sites for swimming and relaxing. However, please pack some light garments as summer rains can be frequent, and thunderstorms are not uncommon.

Autumn (September to November)
Autumn in Berlin delivers a stunning shift to the city's scenery as the leaves change hues and fall. September remains relatively warm, with temperatures between 11°C and 20°C (52°F to 68°F). As the season progresses, October sees colder temperatures ranging from 6°C to 13°C (43°F to 55°F), and by November, temperatures drop further, ranging from 2°C to 7°C (36°F to 45°F).

Tourists in autumn can enjoy the lovely landscapes in parks and the rural environs of Berlin. Additionally, the city's cultural sector comes to life during this season, with several film festivals, art exhibitions, and theater performances.

Winter (December through February)
Winter in Berlin may be cold, with temperatures ranging from -2°C to 4°C (28°F to 39°F) in December, January, and February. Snow is not uncommon during this season, providing a magnificent winter wonderland scene.

Tourists visiting during winter can experience the enchanting Christmas markets, with sellers selling crafts, food, and warm drinks. The city's museums and indoor attractions also offer a warm break from the cold weather.

Conclusion

Berlin's weather is defined by four distinct seasons, each giving a distinctive experience for travelers. Spring delivers moderate weather and blossoming landscapes, while summer gives warmth and a variety of outdoor activities. Autumn gives brilliant foliage and cultural events, and winter creates a pleasant, festive mood. By understanding Berlin's weather throughout the year, travelers may plan their travels accordingly and make the most of this vibrant and culturally rich European metropolis.

Getting Here

Whether you're traveling from within Europe or outside, accessing Berlin is a smooth and delightful journey. Here are the many transit options, vital travel tips, and insights to guarantee a comfortable and memorable vacation in Berlin.

By Air

Berlin features two major international airports: Berlin Tegel Airport (TXL) and Berlin Schönefeld Airport (SXF). Tegel is located northwest of the city center, whereas Schönefeld is situated southeast. Many airlines offer direct flights to these airports from major cities globally. Upon landing, passengers can quickly access the city core via numerous forms of transportation.

Public Transport from Airports: From Tegel Airport, you can take the TXL Express Bus or the X9 bus, which links directly to Berlin's major railway station (Hauptbahnhof) in around 20-30 minutes. Schönefeld Airport is well-connected by the S-Bahn (suburban rail) lines S9 and S45, taking around 30 minutes to reach the city center.

By Train

For those traveling within Europe, train travel to Berlin is a quick and scenic choice. The city is well-connected to several European capitals and large cities through the Deutsche Bahn (DB) network. Berlin Hauptbahnhof, the principal railway station, is an architectural marvel and serves as a gateway to the city. High-speed trains like ICE and EuroCity provide comfortable and efficient travel.

By Car

If you love road travel or have other locations planned, traveling to Berlin can be an appealing choice. Germany's well-maintained autobahn infrastructure enables pleasant and speedy travel. Remember to familiarize yourself with German driving restrictions, including speed limits and environmental zones in the city center. Parking in central Berlin may be tricky and expensive, so utilizing public transport within the city is typically more feasible.

Visa Requirements
Before arranging your trip to Berlin, check you have the essential travel documents. Citizens from the European Union (EU) and the Schengen Area do not require a visa for short stays. Travelers from other countries may however need to apply for a Schengen visa. Check the German embassy or consulate in your native country for up-to-date information and regulations.

Local Transportation
Berlin's efficient public transportation system comprises buses, trams, U-Bahn (underground), and S-Bahn (suburban trains). The BVG (Berliner Verkehrsbetriebe) manages all types of public transit and offers different ticket options, including single tickets, day passes, and multi-day passes. The Berlin Welcome Card is a good alternative for travelers as it allows unrestricted transit and discounts to main attractions.

Conclusion
Reaching Berlin as a tourist is a hassle-free and delightful experience, thanks to its well-connected transportation system and tourist-friendly services. Whether you come by

air, train, or car, the city awaits its rich history, vibrant culture, and amazing experiences that will make a lasting impact on any traveler. Plan your trip properly, embrace the local culture, and get ready to immerse yourself in the enchanting charm of Berlin.

Top Attractions

As one of the most visited cities in Europe, Berlin provides a multitude of activities that cater to all interests. From its famous landmarks to its bustling art scene, here are the must-visit tourist sites in Berlin.

Brandenburg Gate

The Brandenburg Gate, located in the middle of Berlin is an iconic edifice steeped in history and a symbol of the nation's resilience and solidarity. Built in the late 18th century, this neoclassical triumphal arch stands as a symbol of Germany's stormy past and its march toward reunification.

The Brandenburg Gate, known as "Brandenburger Tor" in German, was commissioned by King Frederick William II of Prussia and created by architect Carl Gotthard Langhans.

Construction of Brandenburg Gate began in 1788 and was finished in 1791. The gate is a significant element of the city's history, originally acting as one of the entrance gates to Berlin, marking the beginning of the route going to the city of Brandenburg a der Havel.

Over the years, the gate witnessed key historical events, including Napoleon's capture of Berlin and the division of Germany during the Cold War. During the latter period, the gate became a symbol of the split city, towering ominously near the Berlin Wall, which separated East and West Berlin.

Fall of the Wall and Reunification
The collapse of the Berlin Wall in 1989 was a monumental occurrence that symbolized the end of the Cold War and started a new era for Germany. The Brandenburg Gate, once a symbol of division, became a symbol of optimism and unity. It witnessed exuberant crowds from both sides of the wall enjoying their newfound freedom and the hope of reunification.

Today, the gate stands as a tribute to Germany's triumph over its stormy past. It serves as a powerful reminder of the country's ability to overcome hardships and unite as a nation.

Architectural Significance
The Brandenburg Gate's architectural style exhibits neoclassical influences, inspired by the Propylaea in Athens. The gate includes five pathways, with the central one reserved for royalty during its original use. Doric columns and ornate sculptures adorn the gate, including the famed Quadriga, a chariot propelled by four horses, representing victory.

The gate received considerable reconstruction during World War II and again following the fall of the Berlin Wall. These restorations preserved its historical integrity and assured its continued prominence as a national landmark.

Tourist Experience

As a tourist, visiting the Brandenburg Gate is a necessity for a thorough grasp of Germany's history and culture. The facility is accessible and free to visit, open to the public year-round. Tourists can pass through the gate and explore both sides to comprehend its significance during the Cold War and its subsequent role in German reunification.

Visitors can also attend guided tours or use audio guides to learn about the gate's history and architectural elements. The nearby Pariser Platz offers a wonderful perspective of the gate, making it a popular site for pictures.

Reichstag Building

The Reichstag Building is a historic and iconic edifice that possesses great cultural, political, and architectural importance. It has witnessed the tumultuous history of Germany and stands as a symbol of democracy and endurance.

The Reichstag Building's history may be traced back to the late 19th century when it was created to house the Imperial Diet, the parliament of the German Empire. Designed by architect Paul Wallot, the structure was finished in 1894. However, it suffered serious damage during World War II, particularly during the Battle of Berlin in 1945, leaving it in ruins. After the war, the split city of Berlin had the Reichstag Building positioned in Soviet-controlled East Berlin.

The Reichstag Building shows a blend of architectural styles. The initial design was influenced by the Renaissance and

Baroque periods, with a great dome inspired by the Pantheon in Rome. After its rebuilding following World War II, British architect Sir Norman Foster constructed the modern glass dome, symbolizing the reunification of Germany and providing an excellent example of contemporary architecture peacefully combining with historical elements. The dome is a striking feature, allowing guests to travel on its spiraling staircase to a viewing platform, affording a panoramic view of Berlin.

As a tourist visiting the Reichstag Building, you may expect a great experience. Entrance to the building is free, however previous registration is required for security reasons. Upon arrival, you'll face a security check before ascending the dome. The guided tour takes you through the historical chambers of the Bundestag (the modern-day German Parliament) and provides insights into the nation's political process. Multimedia exhibitions and displays documenting the building's history provide richness to the experience. The highlight of the visit is definitely the dome's ascension, affording breathtaking views of Berlin's cityscape and iconic monuments such as the Brandenburg Gate and the Tiergarten.

Today, the Reichstag Building serves as the seat of the German Bundestag, the lower house of the German Parliament. It represents the core of German democracy and is a striking reminder of the country's democratic principles. The translucent dome and the open plenary chamber embody the concept of a government that is accountable and open to its citizens. It also symbolizes the reunification of East and West Germany and the country's determination to learn from its traumatic past.

In recent years, the Reichstag Building has periodically become a hub of political protests and gatherings, echoing its historical significance as a platform for political expression. While the building itself is open to the public, the plenary meetings are held for the Members of Parliament. However, spectators can still witness debates and discussions via glass walls that provide peeks into the parliamentary sessions.

Berlin Wall Memorial

The Berlin Wall Memorial is a major historical site that recalls the partition of Germany during the Cold War era and stands as a symbol of hope and solidarity for the nation's reunion.

The Berlin Wall was constructed in 1961 by the German Democratic Republic (East Germany) to prevent its residents from escaping to West Berlin, which was under the control of Western powers. The wall spanned around 155 kilometers and contained barriers, watchtowers, and severely defended zones known as the "Death Strip." The memorial protects the last intact pieces of the wall, allowing visitors a genuine view of the past.

One of the important features of the Berlin Wall Memorial is the Documentation Center, which presents a comprehensive exposition of the history of the wall and the division of Berlin. The center incorporates images, videos, personal testimony, and interactive displays that vividly depict the horrific stories of individuals touched by the wall's construction. Tourists can immerse themselves in the storylines of families divided, heroic escape attempts, and the human cost of living under authoritarian tyranny.

Adjacent to the Documentation Center is the open-air memorial site. Here, tourists can explore a preserved stretch of the old wall, replete with watchtowers and the Death Strip. The sharp contrast between the bustling modern city and the vestiges of the wall produces a sad atmosphere, provoking meditation on the significance of the monument.

At the memorial, guests can also visit the Chapel of Reconciliation, a recreation of the original chapel that stood on the site before the wall's construction. The chapel serves as a place of commemoration and reflection, providing a quiet space for visitors to consider the historical events that happened here.

Additionally, the Window of Remembrance is a sad component of the memorial, showing images and biographies of persons who lost their lives attempting to cross the wall. The window serves as a striking reminder of the human toll of the division and the urgency of striving towards unity and peace.

Guided tours are available at the Berlin Wall Memorial, allowing visitors a fuller knowledge of the historical backdrop, personal experiences, and political ramifications surrounding the wall's construction and subsequent destruction. Expert guides provide essential insights, helping tourists connect emotionally with the events of the past and building a sense of empathy and understanding.

The Berlin Wall Memorial also features a visitor center, where guests can access extra information, instructional materials, and historical relics. The site invites visitors to connect with the complex history of the Cold War and gives context for the greater European division during that period.

Checkpoint Charlie

Checkpoint Charlie was one of the most renowned border crossings between East and West Berlin during the Cold War. It carries historical significance as a symbol of the tense split between the communist East and the capitalist West. Today, it serves as a prominent tourist attraction, affording visitors a look into the past and a reminder of the struggles endured during that era.

Checkpoint Charlie was located in the middle of Berlin and operated from 1961 to 1990. It was one of the three border crossings designated for foreigners and diplomats, and its name was drawn from the NATO phonetic alphabet, with "Charlie" symbolizing the letter "C." The other two checkpoints were Checkpoint Alpha at Helmstedt-Marienborn, and Checkpoint Bravo at Dreilinden, both near the West German border.

During the early years of its operation, Checkpoint Charlie was a rather modest wooden building. However, when tensions grew between the United States and the Soviet Union, the checkpoint experienced substantial alterations. In October 1961, the historic stand-off between American and Soviet tanks happened at this checkpoint, increasing global anxieties about the potential outbreak of a nuclear war.

The checkpoint was highly fortified on both sides. On the Eastern side, the East German government created the famed Berlin Wall, a concrete barrier that separated East from West Berlin. It acted as a physical barrier preventing East Berliners from defecting to the West. On the Western side, American soldiers were stationed to handle the crossing of Allied personnel and diplomats.

Today, the area around Checkpoint Charlie has been turned into a historical landmark and open-air museum. Visitors can explore the site, view the recreated guardhouse, and see original relics and exhibits that describe the checkpoint's history. Several museums nearby, such as the Checkpoint Charlie Museum (Mauermuseum), provide greater insights into the stories of those who sought to flee East Berlin and the efforts of various individuals and organizations campaigning against the tyranny of the Wall.

The Checkpoint Charlie Museum includes a collection of things like escape vehicles, documents, and personal accounts of escape attempts, which interest tourists and remind them of the human cost of the split. The museum also gives insight into the many ways utilized to escape, such as tunnels, hidden compartments in vehicles, and daring efforts to pass the Wall under the cover of night.

While Checkpoint Charlie itself is a renowned tourist site, the area surrounding it also offers many restaurants, cafes, and stores. Tourists can enjoy in authentic German food or find mementos relating to the Cold War and Berlin's history.

Visiting Checkpoint Charlie is not simply a historical event but also an emotional one. It serves as a poignant reminder of the atrocities done during the Cold War and the resilience of people who desired freedom. The checkpoint has become a symbol of hope, human determination, and the victory of democracy against authoritarianism.

Museumsinsel

Museumsinsel, commonly known as Museum Island, is a UNESCO World Heritage site, it is a unique cultural complex that comprises five world-renowned museums, each of which shows an extraordinary collection of art and historical items. Visiting Museumsinsel is like taking a journey through time and exploring the cultural treasures of many civilizations.

History Museumsinsel's history extends back to the early 19th century when King Frederick William III of Prussia initiated the construction of the first museum, the Altes Museum, constructed by Karl Friedrich Schinkel. Over the years, new museums were added to the island, including the Neues Museum, the Alte Nationalgalerie, the Bode Museum, and the Pergamon Museum. The island's architectural splendor is as striking as the treasures it houses, making it a cultural and historical monument in Berlin.

Museums Altes Museum: The Altes Museum, or Old Museum, was the first to open its doors in 1830. It is dedicated to ancient art and sculptures, presenting a great collection of Greek, Roman, and Etruscan relics. The museum's neoclassical building adds to the grandeur of the exhibits, offering visitors a unique sense of the past.

Neues Museum: Severely destroyed during World War II, the Neues Museum was repaired and reopened in 2009. This museum houses an astonishing assortment of ancient Egyptian treasures, including the famed bust of Queen Nefertiti. The museum's design, a mix of historic and modern architecture, produces a beautiful synthesis of the past and the present.

Alte Nationalgalerie: For art connoisseurs, the Alte Nationalgalerie is a must-visit. It concentrates on 19th-century art, including Romantic, Neoclassical, and Impressionist masterpieces. The museum's collection comprises works by prominent artists such as Caspar David Friedrich, Adolph Menzel, and Auguste Renoir.

Bode Museum: The Bode Museum is named for its first curator, Wilhelm von Bode, and it is home to an extensive collection of sculptures, Byzantine art, and one of the world's most complete coin collections. The museum's building is an excellent combination of Baroque and Renaissance styles.

Pergamon Museum: The Pergamon Museum is the most visited museum on the island and comprises three main sections: the Collection of Classical Antiquities, the Museum of the Ancient Near East, and the Museum of Islamic Art. The Pergamon Altar, the Ishtar Gate, and the Market Gate of

Miletus are some of the most prominent and awe-inspiring displays within the museum.

Visitor Tips
Ticket Options: It is suggested to get a day pass that provides entrance to all five museums, as each offers a distinct and educational experience. Additionally, it's best to reserve tickets online in advance to prevent long lineups, especially during peak tourist seasons.

Guided Tours: Taking a guided tour can substantially boost your comprehension of the exhibits and the historical relevance of the museums. Many museums offer audio guides or guided tours in multiple languages.

Timing: Given the size of the exhibits, it's tough to see all five museums in one day. Prioritize the museums that interest you the most, or consider spreading your visit across numerous days.

Relaxation Areas: Museumsinsel has wonderful outdoor locations, such as Lustgarten, where you may take a leisurely stroll and observe the architecture and scenery.

Museumsinsel is a treasure mine of art, history, and culture, offering tourists an engaging experience like no other. Exploring this unique island will definitely leave travelers with a profound appreciation for the glories of human imagination and the rich fabric of our shared past.

East Side Gallery

The East Side Gallery is an important and iconic monument in Berlin, commemorating the city's stormy past and the unification of East and West Germany. It is a 1.3-kilometer-long stretch of the Berlin Wall, which previously divided the city during the Cold War. Today, it stands as the longest open-air gallery in the world and a prominent tourist destination.

The Berlin Wall acted as a physical and ideological barrier, separating East Berlin (ruled by the communist German Democratic Republic) as stated earlier from West Berlin (a democratic enclave surrounded by East Germany). The East Side Gallery, founded in 1990, maintained a substantial piece of the wall and repurposed it into a canvas for artists to convey hope, freedom, and unity.

Walking along the East Side Gallery is like wandering through a dramatic and bright art exhibition. Over 100 foreign artists contributed to the 105 paintings that line the wall, giving it an eclectic collection of styles, topics, and messages. Each artwork offers a unique tale, frequently reflecting the creators' feelings, experiences, and viewpoints on freedom, peace, and human rights.

One of the most famous and poignant paintings in the East Side Gallery is "The Fraternal Kiss" by Dmitri Vrubel. This artwork shows the embrace of Soviet leader Leonid Brezhnev and East German President Erich Honecker, symbolizing the political brotherhood between the two countries. However, it also symbolizes the lack of freedom and the harsh nature of their administrations.

Other paintings include scenes of jubilation during the fall of the Berlin Wall, portraits of key personalities, and powerful messages appealing for peace, love, and unity. The gallery's artworks have undergone restoration multiple times to maintain their historical and artistic worth, guaranteeing that future generations can appreciate and learn from this wonderful location.

Visiting the East Side Gallery provides a unique opportunity to immerse oneself in history while simultaneously admiring contemporary art. As you walk along the wall, you can experience the weight of history, visualizing the sharp contrast between the sadness of the divided city and the promise that blossomed following its reunion.

The gallery is accessible to the public year-round, and it is encouraged to visit during daylight hours to properly enjoy the brilliant colors and details of the artwork. There are no entrance fees, allowing everyone to experience this emblem of togetherness and expression freely.

Beyond its artistic value, the East Side Gallery offers stunning views of the Spree River and the adjacent urban landscape. Nearby, travelers may explore the lively Friedrichshain neighborhood, noted for its bright street art, alternative culture, and various cafes and pubs.

As with any major tourist location, it is necessary to be respectful of the artworks and the historical value of the East Side Gallery. Graffiti or graffiti is absolutely prohibited since these actions degrade the artistic accomplishments and the memory of those who fought for freedom during the Cold War.

Charlottenburg Palace

Charlottenburg Palace, commonly known as Schloss Charlottenburg, is a splendid Baroque palace located in the Charlottenburg neighborhood of Berlin. Construction of the palace began in 1695 as a vacation house for Sophie Charlotte, the wife of Frederick I. Over the years, it had various additions and reconstructions, resulting in a variety of architectural styles, including Baroque, Rococo, and Neoclassical. This mix of styles gives the palace a unique and intriguing aspect.

As tourists approach Charlottenburg Palace, they are greeted with a stunning entryway including a vast courtyard and an elegant exterior. The center domed tower, embellished with statues and beautiful carvings, immediately draws one's attention. The lovely gardens surrounding the palace create a calm backdrop, enticing tourists to explore its rich foliage and fine sculptures.

Inside the palace, guests can start on a journey through numerous opulently adorned rooms, each boasting its unique historical value. The Old Palace, which goes back to the late 17th century, holds the beautiful Porcelain Cabinet, showing a magnificent collection of Chinese and Japanese porcelain.

The New Wing, erected during the mid-18th century, illustrates the grandeur of Prussian kings and queens. One of the attractions is the Golden Gallery, an intricately furnished ballroom filled with gold leaf and dazzling chandeliers. The White Hall, a majestic dining hall, is another must-see, with its remarkable stucco embellishments and beautiful ceiling frescoes.

The King's Apartments, Queen's Apartments, and the richly furnished Birch Cabinet provide visitors with a picture of the luxury lifestyle and taste of the Prussian rulers.

One of the most enchanting characteristics of Charlottenburg Palace is its gardens. The Baroque-style garden, influenced by French ideas, contains perfectly placed flowerbeds, attractive sculptures, and a calm lake. The Belvedere Tea House, a lovely pavilion set on a hill, offers breathtaking views of the gardens and the surrounding environment.

Throughout the year, the palace holds many cultural events, concerts, and exhibitions, enriching the whole experience for travelers. The Christmas market held on the palace grounds during the holiday season is particularly popular, allowing tourists a chance to experience a traditional German Christmas.

Memorial to the Murdered Jews of Europe

Designed by architect Peter Eisenman and engineer Buro Happold, the memorial serves as a sobering reminder of the atrocities done during the Holocaust. Opened to the public in 2005, this striking site pays tribute to the millions of Jews and other victims who lost their lives under the Nazi government during World War II. Spanning an area of approximately 4.7 acres, the memorial intends to encourage deep meditation and contemplation among visitors.

The Memorial's design is recognized for its startling simplicity and unique style. It features 2,711 concrete slabs, or stelae, of varied heights set in a grid-like layout over the site. As visitors pass around the memorial, the ground undulates, producing an uncomfortable and disorienting ambiance that evokes the chaos and horror of the Holocaust.

The stelae themselves stand tall and intimidating, signifying the enormity and distinctiveness of each life lost. The structure enables visitors to roam around the maze-like walkways, prompting a spectrum of emotions as they meet the gravity of the catastrophe. As visitors explore deeper into the memorial, the stelae increase in height, further emphasizing the sense of isolation and vulnerability, echoing the horror and misery experienced by the victims during the Holocaust.

The Memorial to the Murdered Jews of Europe acts as a symbol of remembrance and commemoration. It is purposely devoid of obvious symbols, inscriptions, or names, allowing visitors to interpret and personalize their experience. The lack of conventional marks emphasizes the faceless character of the victims' suffering and the elimination of individual identities under Nazi rule.

The grandeur of the memorial also conveys the sheer magnitude of the catastrophe, making it hard to ignore the magnitude of six million lives lost. The play of light and shadows formed by the stelae throughout the day further enhances the emotional impact, expressing hope and resilience among the gloom.

Visiting the Memorial may be a powerful and emotional experience. The immense expanse of stelae stimulates meditation on the scale of the Holocaust, while the convoluted passageways evoke emotions of uncertainty and isolation. The solitude of the place inspires solemn thought and reverence for the victims' remembrance.

As visitors go through the memorial, they may find people seeking solace or indulging in silent thought. The open form allows for private or collective experiences, giving it a location for both personal contemplation and shared sadness.

Adjacent to the Memorial, the Visitor Center provides detailed information about the Holocaust, its historical background, and its impact on individuals and families. Visitors can obtain deeper insights into this sad chapter of history through displays, documents, and testimony, giving educational value to the experience.

Tiergarten

Victory Column

Tiergarten is a spectacular urban park, encompassing an area of around 520 acres, it is one of the largest and most popular green spaces in the city. Its name translates to "Animal Garden" in English, but don't be deceived; the park is much more than just a zoo. Instead, it offers a varied range of attractions and recreational possibilities that cater to both locals and tourists alike.

The Tiergarten's history stretches back to the 16th century when it was first built as a hunting place for the Prussian nobles. Over the ages, it transformed from a private hunting reserve into a public park. During the 18th and 19th centuries, the park received considerable modifications and landscaping under renowned architects and landscapers, changing it into a more accessible and visually beautiful green space for the public to enjoy.

Tiergarten stands as a beautiful refuge amidst the hectic cityscape of Berlin. Its wide meadows, tree-lined avenues, and glistening lakes create an ideal location for leisure and outdoor sports. Locals often gather here to exercise, cycle, hold picnics or simply enjoy leisurely strolls in nature. Visitors seeking a moment of quiet will find refuge in the park's serene ambiance, offering a respite from the metropolitan tumult.

Within Tiergarten, there are various monuments and landmarks of historical and cultural value. The Victory Column (Siegessäule) is undoubtedly the most iconic structure. Additionally, the Soviet War Memorial and the Brandenburg Gate are located nearby, contributing to the park's historical background.

Tiergarten Park also has several sculptures and monuments dispersed around its grounds, each with its own distinct story and artistic value. These artworks enhance the park's attractiveness and cultural appeal.

As indicated before, despite the name "Tiergarten," the park does not primarily host animals. However, the Berlin Zoological Garden, one of the oldest and most recognized zoos globally, is adjacent to Tiergarten and easily accessible to visitors. The zoo is home to a large assortment of animals, making it a fascinating family excursion.

The park offers several recreational activities for individuals of all ages. The huge meadows are great for picnics and sports, while the water bodies draw rowing enthusiasts and boat rentals. Visitors can also join locals in casual games of beach volleyball or simply sunbathe during sunny months.

Tiergarten contains various cafes and restaurants, allowing sufficient possibilities to experience wonderful local food and international delicacies. These cafés offer the perfect spots to unwind after touring the park and enjoy a cup of coffee or a good meal while taking in the surrounding scenery.

Throughout the year, Tiergarten plays host to many events and festivals. From cultural meetings to open-air concerts, the park's broad spaces serve as perfect sites for huge gatherings. Tourists can keep an eye on the local event calendars to see if any festivities overlap with their visit.

Due to its central location, Tiergarten is easily accessible by public transit. Visitors can utilize the S-Bahn, U-Bahn, and buses, or even approach it on foot or by bicycle from many sections of the city. Its proximity to other important sights, such as the Brandenburg Gate and Potsdamer Platz, makes it a must-visit destination for travelers exploring Berlin.

Gendarmenmarkt

Often considered to be the most beautiful square in Berlin, Gendarmenmarkt has a harmonic blend of architectural marvels, cultural institutions, and a bustling environment that attracts both locals and tourists alike.

Originally designed in the late 17th century by Johann Arnold Nering, Gendarmenmarkt was initially called Linden-Markt. In the 18th century, it was named for the cuirassier regiment, the Gens d'Armes, who used to reside there. The area is flanked by three great buildings: the French Cathedral (Französischer Dom), the German Cathedral (Deutscher Dom), and the Concert House (Konzerthaus).

The French Cathedral, constructed by Carl von Gontard, is an awe-inspiring monument with its majestic dome and a lovely façade embellished with Corinthian columns. Opposite it sits the German Cathedral, created by Martin Grünberg, which displays a beautiful Baroque design and includes an exhibition on German legislative history. The Concert House, designed by Karl Friedrich Schinkel, is a neoclassical masterpiece and serves as a venue for world-class concerts and shows.

Gendarmenmarkt is not simply an architectural beauty but also home to notable cultural institutions. The Konzerthaus Berlin, with its excellent acoustics and a rich tradition of presenting great musicians and orchestras, draws music aficionados from around the world. Moreover, the German Cathedral holds the German Historical Museum's permanent exhibition on parliamentary democracy, making it a magnet for history aficionados.

Beyond its architectural magnificence and cultural significance, Gendarmenmarkt offers a bustling and lively ambiance. The square is flanked by attractive cafes, restaurants, and boutiques, making it a perfect spot for relaxing and people-watching. During Christmas time, the area changes into a winter paradise with a delightful Christmas market that attracts locals and tourists alike, offering an array of seasonal delicacies, handicrafts, and mulled wine.

Throughout the year, Gendarmenmarkt organizes a number of events and festivals that add to its charm. Apart from the charming Christmas market, the square also holds the Classic Open Air festival, when world-class musicians perform beneath the open sky, creating a memorable musical experience. Additionally, many cultural events, art exhibitions, and outdoor performances make the plaza a lively and fascinating destination for travelers.

Fernsehturm

Also known as the Berlin TV Tower, is an iconic symbol of Berlin, rising at an astonishing height of 368 meters (1,207 feet), it dominates the city's skyline and gives tourists a unique experience combining history, technology, and spectacular panoramic views.

The Fernsehturm was constructed in the 1960s by the German Democratic Republic (GDR) as a showcase of East German architectural excellence and a symbol of socialist triumph. Its construction began in 1965, and it was completed in 1969. The tower's design, a slender concrete pillar with a spherical observation deck and a rotating restaurant, was a product of the architectural and engineering genius of the period.

Today, the Fernsehturm welcomes millions of people each year who come to see Berlin from its observation decks and enjoy its various attractions. One of the biggest draws for tourists is the observation deck, which offers a breathtaking 360-degree panorama of the city. On clear days, visibility can extend up to 40 kilometers (25 miles), allowing tourists to see iconic monuments like the Brandenburg Gate, the Reichstag building, and the Berlin Cathedral. The vista also creates a dramatic contrast between the historic elegance of the city's old buildings and the modernity of its newer structures.

To enter the observation deck, tourists utilize a high-speed elevator that whisks them to the top in just 40 seconds. The elevator trip itself is an adventure, with the walls composed of glass, offering a sight of the tower's structure as it ascends.

Another feature within the Fernsehturm is the revolving Sphere Restaurant, located right above the observation deck. As the name suggests, the restaurant gently circles, completing a full rotation every hour. This unique feature allows diners to experience a diversified vision of the city while eating a tasty dinner. However, it is advisable to make appointments in advance, as the restaurant tends to be extremely popular and might fill up quickly.

The Fernsehturm is not just an architectural masterpiece but also a tribute to technical innovation. At its time of construction, it was one of the highest structures in the world and a wonder of engineering. Despite its age, it has been regularly renovated and upgraded to keep up with the changing times. Its observation deck currently incorporates interactive touchscreens that provide information about the sites visible from the tower and the history of Berlin.

For history aficionados, a visit to the Fernsehturm also provides a look into the city's past. Built during the height of the Cold War, it symbolizes the political mood of that era and serves as a reminder of Germany's divided history.

DDR Museum

The DDR Museum is an educational site that gives tourists an immersion experience into the history and culture of the German Democratic Republic (GDR). The museum provides a unique opportunity to travel back in time and get insights into the daily lives, political structures, and social dynamics that built this communist state.

The museum's architecture and layout are purposely designed to replicate a typical East German residential building, immediately immersing visitors into the mood of the era. As guests go through the door, they are welcomed by exhibitions that cover a wide range of areas of life in the GDR, including politics, economy, education, housing, and recreation. Each component is painstakingly edited to create a balanced and nuanced portrayal of the time, affording visitors a thorough image of the realities faced by the East German people.

The political component of the DDR Museum looks into the complexity of the ruling Socialist Unity Party of Germany (SED) and the Ministry for State Security (Stasi). Visitors can study the ideology underlying the GDR's administration, propaganda tactics, and the impact of the Berlin Wall on people's lives. They can also study about the rise and fall of Erich Honecker, the General Secretary of the SED and the leader of East Germany during the 1980s.

The museum provides an opportunity to learn the economic structure of the GDR, which was characterized by a planned economy with state-owned firms. Exhibits showcase various facets of daily living, such as shopping in the "Intershop," the government-owned store where luxury products were sold in Western currencies. Visitors can also witness the classic "Trabant" automobile, a symbol of East German manufacture.

Education and culture were highly prized in the GDR, and the museum represents this aspect as well. Visitors can study the educational system, from kindergarten through university, and obtain insights into the state-controlled media and culture, including literature, cinema, and music.

One of the most unique and interactive elements of the DDR Museum is the "Everyday Life" display. Here, visitors can open drawers, sit on furniture, and touch numerous things that were part of everyday life in East Germany. This hands-on method allows travelers to experience the past in a tactile and personal way, producing a memorable and engaging experience.

The museum also exhibits a model of a normal East German apartment, allowing a look into the living conditions and furnishings of an average family during that time. Visitors can compare their own modern lifestyles with the small living areas and rudimentary facilities that were widespread in the GDR.

The DDR Museum's commitment to creating an immersive experience extends to its multimedia displays and interactive projects. Visitors can see the documentary film, listen to personal testimony, and connect with touch-screen displays to obtain a fuller knowledge of the historical backdrop and specific experiences of East Germans.

Berlin Philharmonic

The Berlin Philharmonic, often known as the Berliner Philharmoniker, is one of the world's most prominent and recognized orchestras. It has a long history and plays a crucial part in the city's cultural landscape. Established in 1882, the orchestra has been at the forefront of musical excellence and innovation for almost a century.

The Berlin Philharmonic's home venue is the Philharmonie, a remarkable edifice created by architect Hans Scharoun. The Philharmonie's distinctive architecture sets the audience in a circular seating arrangement surrounding the stage, allowing for excellent acoustics and an intimate connection between musicians and listeners. The building's stunning architecture alone is worth a visit, with its striking tent-like top and golden façade.

Tourists visiting the Berlin Philharmonic can look forward to outstanding musical experiences. The orchestra is noted for its remarkable command of a diverse repertoire, ranging from classical masterpieces to modern works. Conductors of international distinction have led the Berlin Philharmonic over the years, including Herbert von Karajan, Claudio Abbado, and Sir Simon Rattle, among others. Each conductor adds their individual interpretation and style, ensuring that every performance is a distinct and memorable experience.

The Berlin Philharmonic hosts special events and festivals as well, drawing music enthusiasts from around the world. The orchestra's Christmas concerts, New Year's Eve concerts, and the Berliner Philharmoniker's European Concert presented yearly on May 1st in different European towns, are particularly popular. These events exhibit the orchestra's versatility and ability to convey the essence of many musical genres.

One of the most intriguing features of the Berlin Philharmonic is its commitment to innovation and accessibility. The orchestra has embraced technology to reach a greater audience through its Digital Concert Hall. With this internet platform, everyone may enjoy live-streamed performances and a vast archive of concerts from the comfort of their homes. This effort has broadened the orchestra's global reach, allowing individuals from all corners of the world to experience the beauty of the Berlin Philharmonic.

The Berlin Philharmonic's influence goes beyond its musical prowess. It has played a vital role in shaping the city's cultural identity and fostering worldwide cultural exchange. The orchestra routinely embarks on worldwide tours, exhibiting Germany's rich musical history on the global stage. Through its instructional and outreach activities, it also supports the skills of young musicians, contributing to the future of classical music.

For those considering a visit to the Berlin Philharmonic, it is advisable to check the concert calendar in advance and get tickets early, as the demand for their performances is great. Attending a live performance in the renowned Philharmonie is an extraordinary experience that immerses the audience in the realm of classical music at its finest.

Berliner Unterwelten

While most tourists rush to renowned sites such as the Brandenburg Gate and the Berlin Wall, there lies a hidden realm beneath the bustling streets - the Berliner Unterwelten, or Berlin Underworld. This subterranean labyrinth is a fascinating tour into the city's past, spanning its military adventures, the Cold War era, and civilian life during various periods.

The Berliner Unterwelten is a large network of underground chambers, tunnels, bunkers, and shelters that played a crucial part during significant chapters of Berlin's history. Many of these spaces were erected during World War II to serve as air-raid shelters for civilians, offering sanctuary from incessant bombs. These bunkers were crucial lifelines for the population during the stormy years of war, and visiting them offers a remarkable insight into the hardships faced by Berliners during that period.

Tourists wishing to dig into this particular facet of Berlin's past can join in guided excursions offered by the Berliner Unterwelten organization. These excursions, conducted by skilled guides, take tourists on an exciting journey through diverse underground places. The trips are well-organized, and safety measures are in place to provide a memorable yet secure experience.

One of the main trip highlights is the Berliner Unterwelten Museum, which provides an educational starting point. The museum highlights exhibits and memorabilia that offer insight into the building of the bunkers, their function during the war, and the daily lives of citizens who took cover within them. Photographs, personal stories, and interactive exhibits provide a thorough insight into this underground environment.

The Dark Worlds Tour is an outstanding event for history aficionados. It takes visitors into an authentic air-raid shelter, illustrating the hardships endured by civilians during bombing strikes. The darkness, small confines, and eerie silence convey a feeling of the difficulties faced throughout the conflict, producing a truly immersive experience.

Beyond its wartime significance, the Berliner Unterwelten also played a key role during the Cold War. The Ghost Stations Tour offers insight into the unique narrative of the U-Bahn and S-Bahn stations that were located in East Berlin but intersected West Berlin territory. These "ghost stations" were closed down and guarded by military soldiers owing to political tensions, and the trip investigates the remarkable escapes and stories of people who sought to cross these forbidden frontiers.

For the more daring tourists, there are trips that descend inside the huge tunnel systems used for clandestine purposes during the Cold War. Visitors can follow the steps of former spies and feel the excitement of being in the precise areas where secret exchanges and espionage once took place.

The attempts to protect and maintain these underground places deserve credit. The Berliner Unterwelten group, mostly run by volunteers, is dedicated to maintaining these historical sites and informing the public about their relevance. Proceeds from the excursions contribute to the continuing restoration efforts and research.

Topography of Terror

The Topography of Terror is an invaluable historical site that offers a dramatic peek into the worst chapter of German history - the Nazi era. The site was originally the headquarters of the Gestapo, the SS, and the Reich Security Main Office from 1933 to 1945. Today, it exists as a museum and memorial, giving visitors with a thorough and terrifying description of the Nazi regime's horrors.

The physical topography of the location plays a key part in its historical significance. The museum is situated on the former Prinz-Albrecht-Straße, which was previously a prominent location for the Nazi security system. Visitors can tour the historic cellars and foundations of buildings that held key figures of the Nazi government. The display is put out on the remnants of the previous headquarters, preserving its historical authenticity and allowing people to immerse themselves in the tragic history of the area.

Upon entering the museum, guests are presented with a large collection of documents, images, and historical relics. The exhibition gives a historical narrative of the Nazi rise to power, the formation of the totalitarian government, and its influence on people and society as a whole. The museum does not shy away from the atrocities of the past but rather confronts visitors with the terrible reality of the Holocaust, concentration camps, and the systematic persecution of millions of innocent people.

One of the most frightening parts of the Topography of Terror is the intact section of the Berlin Wall that runs along the site's perimeter. This serves as a striking reminder of the divide and misery that transpired in Berlin during the Cold War era. The combination of Nazi history and Cold War relics produces a compelling ambiance, highlighting the significance of the place in establishing modern Germany's identity and commitment to human rights.

Throughout the museum, visitors discover personal stories, biographies, and accounts of individuals who endured under Nazi rule. These anecdotes humanize the statistics and serve as a reminder of the significance of never forgetting the past to prevent similar horrors from happening again. Interactive exhibitions and multimedia installations also offer a greater understanding of the historical background, generating empathy and contemplation among travelers.

The Topography of Terror contains an outdoor space that features panels with detailed information about the former buildings, the main individuals of the regime, and the crimes committed at this place. This open-air display allows visitors to explore at their own speed while soaking in the surroundings where the events unfolded.

The Topography of Terror is more than just a historical place; it functions as a site of recollection and reconciliation. The museum urges visitors to reflect on the repercussions of unbridled power, ideology-driven hate, and the significance of defending democratic ideals and human rights. It also recognizes Germany's responsibility for its past and its determination to ensure such crimes never happen again.

Hackesche Höfe

Hackesche Höfe is a beautiful and dynamic ensemble of eight interlinked courtyards, forming one of the city's most popular attractions. Located in the Mitte area, this historic complex is steeped in history, culture, and creative flare.

Dating back to the early 20th century, Hackesche Höfe was originally erected between 1906 and 1907. The structure was the vision of the architect Kurt Berndt and was commissioned by the forward-thinking Jewish entrepreneur, August Endell. The complex was envisioned as an interconnected sequence of courtyards, bringing together residential spaces, businesses, and cultural events. Despite being devastated during World War II, the complex was eventually repaired and revived, showing a beautiful blend of Jugendstil (Art Nouveau) and industrial architecture.

Hackesche Höfe's architectural beauty is one of its primary draws. As guests arrive in the first courtyard, they are treated to a spectacular display of Jugendstil facades, embellished with elaborate features and brilliant mosaics. Each courtyard reveals something unique, making it a treat to explore. The innovative interlinking of courtyards produces an interesting maze-like experience, adding to the charm and attraction of the site.

The artistic spirit of Hackesche Höfe is obvious. Art galleries, theaters, cafes, and stores may be found throughout the complex. Art fans will be happy to discover the Hackesche Höfe Theater, which displays a broad range of performances, including drama, comedy, and musicals. The courtyards themselves serve as a canvas for street art and graffiti, reflecting Berlin's reputation as a haven for artists and free expression.

For shopping enthusiasts, Hackesche Höfe provides a choice of boutiques and distinctive shops, selling everything from fashion to jewelry, crafts, and souvenirs. The courtyards are home to a mix of famous labels and young designers, making it a hot destination for fashion-forward individuals.

When hunger hits, travelers are spoiled for choice with the range of gastronomic delights offered. From classic German cuisine to international cuisines and innovative eating experiences, the restaurants and cafes in the complex appeal to all interests and budgets. Tourists can relish local specialties or indulge in foreign cuisines while enjoying the vibrant ambiance of the courtyards.

As the sun sets, Hackesche Höfe evolves into a lively nightlife destination. The courtyards come alive with live music, entertainment, and a dynamic atmosphere that goes well into the night. Bars and clubs in and around the neighborhood provide different experiences, from classy cocktail lounges to bohemian dance venues, attracting both locals and tourists alike.

Apart from its architectural beauty, Hackesche Höfe has historical value, since it represents the city's stormy past. During the GDR era, the courtyards fell into ruin, but with the reunification of Germany, the neighborhood saw a regeneration, attracting artists, musicians, and creative minds. Today, it stands as a symbol of Berlin's resilience and creative spirit.

Hackesche Höfe is conveniently accessible by public transit, with the Hackescher Markt S-Bahn station just a short walk away. The area can get rather busy, especially on weekends, so it's better to visit during weekdays for a more calm experience.

Nikolaiviertel

Nikolaiviertel, commonly known as Nikolai Quarter or Nicholas' Quarter dates back to the 13th century when Berlin was initially formed. It is one of the few sections that survived the devastation of World War II, making it an important memorial to the city's past. The district receives its name from the majestic St. Nicholas' Church, which stands as a centerpiece and is the oldest church in Berlin. Tourists can explore the church and its crypt, learning about its significance in Berlin's history.

The district is known for its picturesque medieval-style architecture, having cobblestone streets, tiny lanes, and classic red-brick buildings. Many of the structures have been meticulously restored to their former splendor, affording tourists a glimpse into Berlin's architectural legacy. The area's ambiance takes travelers on a voyage back in time, allowing them to envision what life was like centuries ago.

Nikolaiviertel is home to various museums and art galleries that provide a deeper insight into Berlin's past and present. The Ephraim-Palais, a Baroque-style palace, houses a museum that highlights Berlin's history and cultural growth. Art enthusiasts will appreciate the art shows that often take place in the galleries dotted across the area.

Nikolaiviertel is also an excellent destination for shopping, with many boutique boutiques offering unusual souvenirs, crafts, and traditional German products. Tourists can find homemade souvenirs, artisanal goods, and local artwork, making it a great destination to pick up unforgettable keepsakes from their Berlin trip.

Throughout the year, Nikolaiviertel hosts many events and festivals that display its cultural heritage and community spirit. The Christmas market in December is particularly enchanting, with festive decorations, seasonal food, and a magical ambiance that captures the holiday mood.

The district's location along the banks of the River Spree adds to its appeal. Tourists can take leisurely boat cruises along the river, affording new viewpoints of Berlin's sights and gorgeous surroundings. A boat excursion is a fantastic way to unwind after touring the streets and museums of Nikolaiviertel.

Nikolaiviertel is strategically positioned near other main sights in Berlin, making it easily accessible for travelers. Visitors can explore neighboring landmarks such as the Berlin Cathedral, Museum Island, and Alexanderplatz, all within walking distance.

Berlinische Galerie

Berlinische Galerie is a renowned art museum established in 1975, the museum is situated in the dynamic district of Kreuzberg and is committed to displaying the artistic history of Berlin and its cultural evolution from the 19th century to the present day.

The museum's collection includes a diverse array of art mediums, including paintings, sculptures, photography, prints, multimedia installations, and architectural projects. The focus on Berlin's art and cultural history allows visitors to obtain insights into the city's dynamic artistic growth over time. The galleries are expertly organized, providing a chronological and thematic organization that allows an immersive experience.

As a tourist, you will have the option to explore numerous areas of the museum, each dedicated to certain times and movements. The 19th-century section offers an insight into

Berlin's artistic scene during the Romantic era and the rise of impressionism. Visitors can examine works by painters like Adolph Menzel, a famous character in German Realism, who caught the spirit of the city in his vivid and vibrant paintings.

Moving into the 20th century, the museum's collection dives into the avant-garde movements that swept through Berlin. The expressionist works of painters such as Ernst Ludwig Kirchner and Emil Nolde illustrate the raw emotions and experimental styles of this period. Additionally, the museum's holdings from the Weimar Republic era exhibit the blooming of artistic innovation amidst a volatile political setting.

The Berlinische Galerie also dedicates space to the Neue Sachlichkeit (New Objectivity) movement, which flourished in the 1920s and 1930s. This movement tried to reflect the objective reality of the world following the devastation of World War I. Works from painters like Otto Dix and George Grosz provide visitors with compelling societal comments and insights into the human condition.

One of the features of the museum is its remarkable collection of photography. From early 20th-century pioneers like Helmar Lerski to contemporary photographers, the Berlinische Galerie highlights the medium's evolution and its significance in capturing the city's history and transition.

Apart from the permanent collection, the museum presents temporary exhibitions that showcase contemporary artists, cutting-edge installations, and novel art forms. These shows provide viewers with a chance to engage with current trends and developments in the art world.

For architecture fans, the Berlinische Galerie exhibits an intriguing collection of architectural drawings, models, and photographs. These objects provide insights into the changing urban landscape of Berlin and the unique architectural styles that have influenced the city's identity.

The museum's dedication to encouraging artistic dialogue extends beyond its exhibition halls. It offers a varied range of educational activities, including seminars, lectures, and guided tours, providing visitors with a deeper knowledge of the artworks and their historical contexts.

Tempelhofer Feld

Tempelhofer Feld is a gigantic public park encompassing over 300 hectares and is one of the world's largest inner-city open spaces, offering a varied range of leisure activities and serving as a living witness to Berlin's past and present. Originally an airbase, Tempelhof Airport played a significant role during World War II and the Berlin Airlift in 1948-1949. After the airport's shutdown in 2008, the area was turned into a public park, maintaining its famous runways, hangars, and historical buildings. Today, visitors can observe the vestiges of this crucial historical period while enjoying the park's recreational attractions.

Tempelhofer Feld is a refuge of greenery amidst the bustling metropolis of Berlin. The huge open space gives locals and tourists alike sufficient opportunities to unwind and connect with nature. The park's large expanses are suitable for leisurely strolls, picnics, and numerous outdoor activities, making it a popular destination for families, couples, and people seeking a calm retreat from city life.

The park's flat and well-maintained runways make it a perfect site for cycling and skating enthusiasts. Tourists can ride bikes from adjacent rental stations or bring their own to explore the immensity of Tempelhofer Feld at a leisurely pace. Skaters can also enjoy the freedom of the open space to perform tricks and maneuvers.

The park's vast fields are great for kite flying. On a windy day, colorful kites fill the sky, producing a beautiful display for both players and spectators. Additionally, the park's broad meadows give adequate room for picnics, affording a perfect opportunity to sample local delicacies or exotic pleasures while soaking in the sunshine.

Tempelhofer Feld boasts various communal gardens where locals raise their food and flowers. This urban gardening effort adds an aspect of sustainability and community engagement to the park. Tourists can observe the inventiveness of Berlin's people and learn about the city's ecological efforts. Additionally, special barbeque sites allow guests to experience the German custom of grilling and having a great day outside.

Throughout the year, Tempelhofer Feld organizes a range of cultural and recreational activities, attracting locals and tourists alike. From music festivals and open-air concerts to sporting events and cultural displays, there's always something going on in the park. Tourists should check the event schedule to discover if any intriguing activities overlap with their visit.

Tempelhofer Feld is notably dog-friendly, letting visitors bring their furry friends along for a day of fun and frolic. The wide-open spaces allow adequate opportunity for dogs to run freely, making it a pleasurable outing for both canines and their owners.

Mauerpark

Mauerpark is a vibrant and historically significant park as well, spanning over 15 hectares. The name "Mauerpark" translates to "Wall Park," which reflects its distinctive historical heritage. During the division of Berlin by the Berlin Wall (1961-1989), this area was part of the death strip. After the fall of the Wall, Mauerpark developed as a symbol of unity and reconciliation. Today, portions of the Wall can still be seen within the park, affording tourists a sobering reminder of Germany's past.

Despite its historical significance, Mauerpark is mostly known for its green spaces and recreational activities. The park offers beautiful meadows, attractive trees, and a delightful rose garden, providing a nice respite from the bustling metropolis. Locals and tourists alike travel to Mauerpark, especially during warm months, to have picnics, relax, and enjoy the natural splendor.

One of the biggest attractions in Mauerpark is the busy flea market that takes place every Sunday. Stretching along the park's walkways, the market provides an eclectic variety of things, including vintage apparel, handcrafted crafts, antique furniture, vinyl records, and unique souvenirs. It's a treasure trove for anyone seeking original Berlin memorabilia and one-of-a-kind stuff. Visitors can also partake in wonderful street food from various stalls, making it a veritable haven for bargain hunters and foodies alike.

Perhaps the most recognizable element of Mauerpark is the colorful open-air singing sessions that occur every Sunday afternoon. At the amphitheater, people congregate to demonstrate their singing talents, turning the park into a lively spectacle. Whether you're a singer or a spectator, the karaoke experience is an amazing thrill, establishing a sense of togetherness among the diverse crowd.

Apart from karaoke, Mauerpark hosts various street entertainment, such as musicians, dancers, and circus acts. These impromptu acts bring an element of surprise and pleasure to tourists' experiences, making every visit unique.

An offshoot of the usual karaoke sessions is the famed Bearpit Karaoke event, which takes place at the amphitheater during the summer months. This particular event attracts a big crowd, and contestants get to sing in front of thousands of people. It has acquired an international reputation and has become one of Berlin's most popular and eccentric attractions.

Mauerpark offers various alternatives for pleasure and sports. There are volleyball fields, basketball courts, and table tennis tables placed throughout the park, allowing both locals and tourists a chance to engage in friendly tournaments and be active.

Mauerpark has evolved into a center for the city's cultural life. Numerous events, concerts, and festivals are conducted here, ranging from music performances to art exhibitions and theater acts. The park acts as a meeting spot for people of different origins, establishing a sense of community and inclusivity.

Treptower Park

Nestled along the banks of the River Spree, Treptower Park encompasses over 88 hectares, this beautiful paradise provides a getaway from the frenetic city life while affording an insight into Berlin's intriguing past likewise.

Treptower Park possesses considerable historical relevance as a memorial site and a symbol of remembering. In the middle of the park is the Soviet War Memorial, a stunning monument honoring the Soviet soldiers who lost during World War II. The memorial, completed in 1949, contains a tall statue of a Soviet soldier clutching a child and a spectacular colonnade with elaborate mosaics depicting episodes from the conflict. The melancholy tone of this site inspires study and reflection on the sacrifices made during one of the worst episodes in history.

Beyond the Soviet War Memorial, Treptower Park provides a myriad of attractions. The lovely grounds are great for leisurely strolls, picnics, and sunbathing. The park's center promenade is surrounded by cherry trees that explode into vivid hues during the spring bloom, producing a captivating spectacle for visitors.

One of the park's primary highlights is Treptower Park Island, a picturesque island within the Spree River that can be reached via the Abteibrücke bridge. The island's quiet environment makes it a good site for pleasant walks and gives spectacular views of the city's cityscape.

For those interested in architecture, the spectacular Insel der Jugend (*Youth Island*) is a must-visit. This island includes Jugendhaus, a magnificently preserved Jugendstil building from the early 20th century. Nowadays, the Jugendhaus functions as a cultural center hosting concerts, exhibitions, and events, adding to the dynamic ambiance of the park.

Treptower Park appeals to sports fans and families alike. Visitors can rent rowing boats or paddleboats to explore the Spree River or simply rest on the riverbank and enjoy the calm setting. The park has well-maintained bike pathways that are great for biking, rollerblading, or having a leisurely stroll.

Moreover, the park is equipped with various playgrounds for youngsters, making it a fantastic alternative for families wishing to spend a fun-filled day outside. Additionally, huge open spaces provide adequate room for picnics, frisbee games, or simply lying down and enjoying the verdant surroundings.

Throughout the year, Treptower Park holds a variety of cultural events and festivals. From music concerts and outdoor theater performances to food festivals and open-air markets, the park offers an intriguing calendar of activities that cater to varied tastes. Tourists visiting during these events get an opportunity to immerse themselves in Berlin's dynamic cultural scene while enjoying the natural beauty of the park.

A trip to Treptower Park wouldn't be complete without experiencing some of the local gastronomic delicacies. The park's surroundings include various cafes, food stalls, and beer gardens where tourists may indulge in typical German cuisine and beverages. The beer gardens, in particular, offer an ideal area to unwind and appreciate a nice brew while watching the world go by.

Berlin Dungeon

The Berlin Dungeon gives visitors a unique and immersive experience, delving into the darker and more horrific aspects of Berlin's history. The Berlin Dungeon takes visitors on a journey through time, experiencing numerous times and events that have shaped the city's past. With a blend of history, storytelling, live actors, and special effects, the attraction gives an intriguing and participatory approach to learning more about Berlin's rich and often scary history.

Upon entering the Berlin Dungeon, tourists are met by costumed performers who create the tone for the encounter. The attraction is organized into various themed rooms or settings, each concentrating on distinct historical times and events. Some of the memorable sequences include the Plague Doctor's laboratory, the torture chamber of the Middle Ages, the horrors of the Thirty Years' War, and the notorious courtroom of the medieval Inquisition.

Throughout the experience, real performers depict individuals from the city's past, from ruthless executioners to condemned inmates. Their captivating performances make the stories come alive, bringing a sense of realism and excitement to the voyage. Visitors can observe historical reenactments and even become part of the production, as actors may call upon volunteers from the crowd to participate in specific scenarios.

Special effects play a key role in enriching the overall experience. With state-of-the-art technology, the Berlin Dungeon generates an atmosphere of horror and suspense. From unexpected dives in the dark to simulated earthquakes, the attraction effectively immerses guests in the events unfolding around them. These effects not only heighten the entertainment value but also contribute to the educational side, allowing visitors to grasp historical events from a more visceral perspective.

While the Berlin Dungeon wants to delight and thrill, it also aims to educate. Behind the theatrical performance lies a foundation of well-researched historical truths. The attraction highlights some of the most significant and gruesome occurrences in Berlin's history, shining light on the city's darker moments. Visitors leave not only with a sense of excitement but also with a deeper appreciation of the struggles and tribulations that Berlin and its citizens suffered.

It is vital to mention that the Berlin Dungeon may not be suitable for everyone. The attraction combines aspects of horror, and some sequences can be powerful or disturbing, particularly for small children or people with a sensitive disposition. However, the organizers provide clear warnings regarding the content and allow people to abandon the event if they find it too overwhelming.

Overall, the Berlin Dungeon offers a fascinating and unforgettable experience for those wishing to understand Berlin's history from a fresh perspective. The interactive nature of the attraction, together with the talents of the live performers and amazing special effects, create a mesmerizing environment that sweeps visitors into the past. Beyond the entertainment element, the Berlin Dungeon succeeds in bringing to light the darker chapters of Berlin's history, ensuring that the memory of these events lives on in the minds of its guests.

As with any tourist attraction, it is important to visit the official (www.thedungeons.com/berlin/en/) website or contact the Berlin Dungeon directly for the most up-to-date information on opening hours, ticket costs, and any age or health restrictions. By doing so, tourists may ensure they have a fully fun and instructive experience during their visit to the Berlin Dungeon.

Clärchens Ballhaus

Clärchens Ballhaus is an iconic wealthy dance hall, founded in 1913 by Fritz Bühler, it has weathered the test of time and is one of the city's most beloved cultural treasures. Clärchens Ballhaus has witnessed almost a century of German history, making it a living museum of the city's past. Originally built as a tiny garden pavilion in the 19th century, it was renovated into a ballroom by Fritz Bühler in the early 20th century. Throughout its existence, the venue has passed through numerous eras, including the Golden Twenties, the grim days of World War II, the partition and reunification of Berlin, and its restoration as a symbol of resistance and cultural preservation.

The building of Clärchens Ballhaus retains the beauty of the past, including a mix of Art Nouveau and neo-baroque styles. The façade still displays its original charm, while the interiors have been meticulously refurbished to keep its historic characteristics. The magnificent chandeliers, polished oak floors, and enormous mirrors create an ambiance that transports visitors back in time, allowing them to experience the elegance and opulence of the past.

At Clärchens Ballhaus, everyone can discover their groove. The dance hall offers a multitude of dancing activities, ranging from conventional ballroom and swing to Latin and modern dance genres. Whether you're a seasoned dancer or an enthusiastic novice, you'll find a perfect event to participate in. The facility also conducts dancing courses and workshops, making it a great spot for tourists to learn new dance skills and engage with locals in a warm and casual environment.

Clärchens Ballhaus comes alive with live music and performances, delivering a real sense of Berlin's cultural life. Local bands and musicians frequently visit the stage, playing a variety of genres that cater to varied preferences. From traditional German tunes to jazz and modern pop, the performances bring an added layer of liveliness to the dance hall's ambiance, assuring an unforgettable experience for visitors.

No cultural excursion is complete without indulging in local food. Clärchens Ballhaus offers a comfortable restaurant with a cuisine that combines classic German meals and cosmopolitan delights. Tourists can enjoy exquisite meals accompanied by a selection of German beers and wines. It's an opportunity to sample classic cuisine while embracing the warmth of German hospitality.

Clärchens Ballhaus is a place where people from all walks of life come together to dance, mingle, and celebrate life. Its friendly and welcoming climate attracts inhabitants and visitors of all ages, producing a true melting pot of cultures and tales. Engaging with the welcoming regulars and employees can offer tourists a deeper knowledge of Berlin's dynamic past and present, building important connections and lasting experiences.

The resilience of Clärchens Ballhaus is a testament to its value as a cultural institution in Berlin. It survived several hurdles throughout its existence, including damage from World War II and the fear of demolition during the city's post-reunification rebuilding. Its continued presence is a reminder of the city's dedication to conserving its legacy and building a feeling of community through shared experiences.

Berliner Dom Museum

Berlin Cathedral

The Berliner Dom Museum, commonly known as the Berlin Cathedral Museum, is a notable cultural institution located within the Berliner Dom (Berlin Cathedral) complex. The museum provides visitors with a thorough and enriching experience by presenting a varied range of items and exhibits that illustrate the history, architecture, and religious significance of the cathedral and its surroundings.

The Berliner Dom itself is an iconic emblem of Berlin and a good example of late 19th-century architecture. The museum, housed within the cathedral's interior, provides visitors with significant insights into the building's history and progress. The cathedral was originally established in the mid-18th century and has undergone substantial modifications and expansions over the years. The museum's exhibits chronologically present the architectural changes, allowing visitors an insight into the cathedral's growth through different centuries.

One of the museum's primary attractions is its collection of religious items and ecclesiastical treasures. These treasures include intricately constructed religious robes, vintage chalices, ornate crucifixes, and old texts. The collection allows visitors to examine the rich religious past of the Berliner Dom and its importance in German Protestantism.

The museum's exhibits also offer light on the cathedral's significance in numerous historical events. Berlin has been a vital participant in the stormy history of Germany, and the Berliner Dom has observed and experienced countless critical occasions. Through multimedia displays, visitors may delve into the cathedral's importance during times of conflict, reunification, and cultural revival, making it a crucial site for history buffs.

For individuals interested in the arts, the Berliner Dom Museum offers a range of paintings, sculptures, and decorative artworks. These pieces, largely from the 19th and early 20th centuries, showcase the aesthetic achievements of German painters and their connection to the cathedral. Visitors can enjoy the wonderful craftsmanship of these objects and obtain a clearer knowledge of the cultural value they possess.

Moreover, the museum periodically offers temporary exhibitions that cater to varied interests. These exhibitions could focus on numerous themes like archaeology, contemporary art, or the effect of the Berliner Dom on pop culture. The dynamic nature of these shows keeps the museum experience new and intriguing for returning visitors.

To complement the tourist experience, the Berliner Dom Museum also provides guided tours led by knowledgeable and dedicated experts. These tours provide a better appreciation of the exhibits and architecture while allowing an opportunity to ask questions and connect with specialists who can provide useful insights.

The Berliner Dom Museum also has an outstanding collection of interactive exhibitions and multimedia works. Through virtual reality experiences and augmented reality technologies, visitors may study the cathedral's historical events and architectural components in an immersive and fascinating manner. This innovative approach to museum curating ensures that visitors of all ages may enjoy and learn from the displays.

Stasi Museum

The Stasi Museum is an essential visit for history aficionados and tourists interested in delving into the clandestine realm of espionage and surveillance during the Cold War era. Housed in the former headquarters of the Ministry for State Security (Ministerium für Staatssicherheit), commonly known as the Stasi, this museum offers a thorough and compelling insight into the East German secret police and its impact on society.

The museum's principal attraction is the building itself. The former Stasi headquarters nicknamed the "House of Ministries," is a vast and intimidating facility that originally housed the centralized leadership of the GDR's secret police. The vast scale of the facility is a tribute to the extent of control and influence the Stasi exercised during its existence. As visitors approach the building, they are immediately struck by its austere and intimidating front, setting the tone for the journey within.

The Exhibits

Upon visiting the museum, visitors are transported back in time to the height of the Cold War. The exhibitions are professionally selected, and each area presents a distinct perspective on the Stasi's actions. The displays incorporate genuine papers, images, surveillance equipment, and personal things, making the experience both immersive and sad.

History and Origins: This section traces the emergence of the Stasi and its origins in the Soviet occupation zone of Germany following World War II. Visitors will obtain insights into Stasi's goal, organizational structure, and the major figures that affected its operations.

Monitoring and Spying Techniques: One of the most interesting features of the exhibit is its portrayal of Stasi's massive monitoring apparatus. Visitors can witness a vast assortment of espionage gadgets, including concealed cameras, wiretaps, and bugging devices used to watch residents' every move, even within their houses.

Repression and Control: The museum doesn't shy away from the evil aspect of the Stasi's operations. It gives insight into the methods of control and repression deployed by the secret police to quiet dissent and stifle opposition. Personal testimonies of victims and survivors add a personal flavor to these depressing presentations.

The Impact on Society: This section discusses how the Stasi's actions affected numerous sectors of East German society, from political protest and creative expression to family dynamics. Visitors can obtain a profound appreciation of the terror and paranoia that permeated everyday life under the watchful eye of the Stasi.

Interactive Elements
To enhance the learning experience, the museum combines interactive components, including audio guides, multimedia presentations, and videos containing conversations with former Stasi operatives and individuals who lived under surveillance. These aspects offer depth to the exhibits, making the past more accessible and relatable to visitors.

Guided Tours and Educational Programs
The Stasi Museum offers guided tours led by trained experts, providing invaluable insights into the historical background and value of the exhibits. Additionally, the museum conducts educational programs for school groups and others seeking a more in-depth understanding of the Stasi's actions and their repercussions.

Reflection and Contemplation
The Stasi Museum is not merely a collection of relics; it is a place for reflection and contemplation. As visitors browse the exhibitions, they are urged to consider the broader ethical problems surrounding state monitoring, individual freedoms, and the role of power in society.

Hamburger Bahnhof

Hamburger Bahnhof - Museum für Gegenwart (Hamburger Bahnhof - Museum for Contemporary Art) is a prominent art museum, built in a historic structure that previously served as one of the city's first train stations, giving it its distinctive name. Today, it serves as a notable example of repurposing industrial architecture for cultural purposes.

Originally erected in 1846, Hamburger Bahnhof was designed by Friedrich Neuhaus as the terminus for the railway line connecting Berlin and Hamburg. The station played a vital part in the construction of Berlin's transportation network during the 19th and early 20th centuries. However, as the city's transportation demands evolved, the station's relevance faded, and it finally fell into neglect.

In 1984, following substantial restorations and modernization, the building was reopened as the Museum for Contemporary

Art. Architect Josef Paul Kleihues directed the conversion, skilfully merging the traditional architectural components with contemporary design, producing a perfect place for the display of modern art.

Hamburger Bahnhof focuses on contemporary art, having a remarkable collection that spans numerous genres, including paintings, sculptures, photos, installations, and multimedia works. The collection comprises works by internationally recognized artists, as well as new talents, making it a dynamic and ever-evolving expression of modern creativity.

Visitors can expect to encounter pieces from influential movements such as Abstract Expressionism, Pop Art, Conceptual Art, and Minimalism. Moreover, the museum houses a comprehensive collection of works from key artists like Andy Warhol, Joseph Beuys, Anselm Kiefer, and Cy Twombly. The richness of the collection allows visitors to study diverse artistic forms and engage with various cultural views.

Hamburger Bahnhof also holds recurring exhibitions that often examine contemporary themes, societal challenges, and experimental forms of artistic expression. These temporary exhibitions give a fresh and thought-provoking experience for repeat visitors and cater to the interests of art lovers and casual tourists alike.

The museum's architectural renovation left it with various distinct exhibition areas that enrich the overall visiting experience. The vast main hall, with its great vaulted ceiling, provides an awe-inspiring environment for large-scale installations and sculptures. The juxtaposition of modern art against the historical backdrop produces a captivating contrast, adding to the museum's special charm.

Adjacent to the main hall, the Rieckhallen offers additional exhibition space, enabling the museum to present various shows simultaneously. The Rieckhallen's industrial aspect, preserved from the building's railway station days, provides a sense of authenticity to the modern artworks presented within.

As the contemporary art scene continues to grow, Hamburger Bahnhof stays committed to keeping at the forefront of innovation in the art world. The museum actively connects with the local and international art community, creating partnerships and exchanges with artists, curators, and institutions worldwide.

Moreover, Hamburger Bahnhof focuses a great emphasis on education and public engagement. Through guided tours, seminars, lectures, and educational activities, the museum attempts to deepen visitors' understanding and appreciation of contemporary art, making it accessible to individuals of all ages and backgrounds.

Friedrichshain Volkspark

Märchenbrunnen

Friedrichshain Volkspark, frequently called simply Volkspark Friedrichshain, is a charming and historically significant public park located in the Friedrichshain area. Covering an area of approximately 49 hectares, the park provides visitors with a lovely blend of nature, recreational amenities, and cultural sites, making it a must-visit destination for both locals and tourists alike.

Established in 1848, Volkspark Friedrichshain bears the distinction of being the oldest public park in Berlin. Its creation was inspired by the English garden movement, which sought to incorporate parts of nature into urban spaces for the benefit of the public. The park's history is entwined with the city's own, having undergone different modifications throughout the years.

One of the park's most recognizable attractions is the fairy-tale-like Märchenbrunnen, or Fairy Tale Fountain, situated near the main entrance. This magnificent fountain, created in 1913, showcases many figures from the Brothers Grimm's fairy tales, and it serves as a beloved meeting area for families and friends. The Märchenbrunnen is a wonderful site to start a leisurely stroll through the park's enchanting trails.

As tourists travel further into Volkspark Friedrichshain, they will find themselves surrounded by lush foliage, wide meadows, and quiet ponds. The park's diverse landscape offers an opportunity for relaxation and pleasure. Whether it's enjoying a picnic on the grass, reading a book beneath the shade of trees, or having a jog along the well-maintained pathways, there is something for everyone to enjoy. For those interested in history, the park also has various monuments and memorials that offer insights into Germany's past.

Sports enthusiasts will be thrilled to discover a selection of facilities accessible in Volkspark Friedrichshain. The park contains tennis courts, volleyball courts, and a skating rink, providing many chances for guests to engage in physical activities. Additionally, there is a huge playground for children, equipped with swings, slides, and climbing frames, guaranteeing that the park is a family-friendly location.

Volkspark Friedrichshain also holds many cultural events and concerts throughout the year. From open-air cinema screenings to music festivals, the park becomes a buzzing focus of cultural activity. Tourists visiting during these events can experience the colorful atmosphere and immerse themselves in Berlin's active arts scene.

Moreover, the park's favorable position makes it easily accessible via public transportation. Visitors can make use of the well-connected Berlin transportation network to reach the park, making it a suitable destination for a day excursion or a calm afternoon break from the hectic metropolis.

Conclusion

From historical landmarks and museums to art, music, and outdoor areas, the city promises a remarkable experience that combines its rich history with its dynamic modern culture. Whether you're interested in researching the past or immersing yourself in contemporary life, Berlin has plenty to offer every traveler. These attractions provide a combination of history, culture, nature, and entertainment, making Berlin a city that appeals to all interests and tastes.

Top Cuisine to Try Out

Berlin is not only recognized for its rich history, culture, and arts but also for its unique and mouth-watering cuisine scene. From classic German cuisine to foreign pleasures, Berlin provides a diverse selection of flavors that cater to all tastes and preferences. For any adventurous food-loving tourist, sampling these delicacies is a necessity to properly experience the city's gastronomic treasures. Here are some popular dishes to sample while visiting Berlin:

Currywurst

Currywurst consists of sliced pork sausage, slathered in a rich tomato-based sauce and generously sprinkled with curry powder, providing a perfect combination of German and Indian flavors.

The origins of Currywurst may be traced back to post-World War II Berlin, notably in 1949, when Herta Heuwer, a Berliner, cleverly mixed ketchup, Worcestershire sauce, and curry powder to create this now-famous sauce. It was an instant smash, and since then, Currywurst has become a vital part of Berlin's street food scene, occupying a particular place in the affections of both locals and tourists alike.

Finding a Currywurst stall in Berlin is as easy as spotting the trademark yellow and red umbrella that generally denotes its presence. The sausage itself is normally produced from pork, but you may also find versions utilizing beef or veal, satisfying varied dietary needs. After grilling or frying the sausage to perfection, it is neatly sliced and served on a paper tray or a small plate, making it an ideal on-the-go lunch or snack while touring the city's various neighborhoods.

The sauce is the soul of the Currywurst, and every vendor has their own recipe, making each experience slightly unique. The tomato-based sauce delivers a tangy and moderately sweet flavor, while the curry powder adds a warm and aromatic kick. The level of spiciness can be modified to suit different tastes, with settings ranging from mild to super spicy. For those who want a vegan or vegetarian option, many sellers now provide plant-based sausages and other sauce alternatives, guaranteeing that everyone can experience this Berlin classic.

The ultimate way to enjoy Currywurst is with a side of crispy and golden-brown fries, forming the classic "Currywurst mit Pommes" combo. Some vendors may also offer bread rolls to make it into a Currywurst sandwich. To complete the experience, locals often wash down the meal with a cool soft drink or a locally brewed beer, improving the enjoyment of this famous comfort dish.

While Currywurst can be found across Germany, experiencing this delicacy in its birthplace, Berlin, offers an authentic experience that connects tourists with the city's culture, history, and culinary traditions. For tourists, Currywurst stalls are dispersed throughout Berlin, from street corners to food markets, and some have even achieved international reputations for their exceptional taste and legacy.

Döner Kebab

Döner Kebab, an iconic dish originating from Turkey, has become a treasured mainstay in Berlin's lively culinary scene. Döner Kebab normally comprises luscious layers of seasoned meat, traditionally beef, lamb, or chicken, which are layered and grilled on a vertical rotisserie. The meat is slow-cooked, allowing the outer layers to become crispy while retaining juiciness. In recent years, versions catering to vegetarians and vegans have also evolved, giving falafel or grilled veggies as a wonderful alternative.

A crucial element of Döner Kebab's attractiveness lies in the specific blend of spices used to marinade the meat. This combination may vary from one vendor to another, bringing a unique touch to each meal. Common spices include cumin, coriander, paprika, garlic, and onion powder, which infuse the meat with a delectable scent and a burst of flavors.

Once cooked, the thinly sliced beef is frequently served in a flatbread called "Fladenbrot" or pita, along with fresh veggies and a range of condiments. Common toppings include shredded lettuce, crunchy cabbage, juicy tomatoes, and sliced onions. A selection of sauces, including the classic yogurt-based tzatziki or spicy harissa, further enhances the experience, allowing guests to tailor their Döner Kebab to suit their taste preferences.

One of the best elements about consuming Döner Kebab in Berlin is the abundance of street food sellers and restaurants selling this tasty delicacy. While it may be found across the city, some neighborhoods are particularly famed for their Döner Kebab offerings, such as Mehringdamm in Kreuzberg or Kottbusser Tor in Neukölln. These spots generally cater to late-night revelers, making it a popular post-party snack.

Apart from its wonderful taste, Döner Kebab also shows Berlin's cultural diversity and history of immigration. It was introduced to the city by Turkish immigrants in the 1970s and has since become a vital element of Berlin's culinary identity. As a result, the dish not only satisfies gourmet needs but also offers a view into the city's heterogeneity.

Eisbein

Eisbein, also known as Schweinshaxe, is a pork knuckle or hock, specifically from the rear leg of a pig. The name "Eisbein" literally translates to "ice leg," which could appear strange at first. However, the term "Eis" in this case refers to the pickling procedure that was previously employed to preserve the meat before refrigeration was commonly available. Nowadays, Eisbein is no longer pickled, but the name has survived, paying homage to its culinary beginnings.

To produce Eisbein, the pig knuckle is first brined or marinated to increase its flavor and suppleness. It is then commonly boiled or roasted until the skin becomes crispy, and the meat is tender and delectable. The dish is commonly served with classic German sides, such as sauerkraut, mashed or boiled potatoes, and a big dollop of mustard.

Berlin's affinity with Eisbein runs deep, and many traditional German restaurants, such as "Gasthäuser" or "Brauereien," proudly feature it on their menus. These venues offer a warm and welcoming ambiance, often furnished with rustic characteristics, offering tourists an authentic German eating experience.

Schnitzel

A journey to this dynamic German metropolis would not be complete without eating this classic meal. Schnitzel refers to a breaded and fried cutlet, primarily made with veal, although pork or chicken varieties are also popular.

The dish's origins may be traced back to the Austrian and German countries, where it has become a timeless classic over the decades. The German name "Schnitzel" translates to "cutlet" in English, which appropriately characterizes the major component of this dish - a thin, tenderized slice of meat that is covered in flour, egg, and breadcrumbs before being fried till golden brown.

In Berlin, you'll discover various restaurants and eateries selling Schnitzel, each giving its unique variation on the original recipe. The city's diversified culinary scene means that you can savor classic Schnitzel varieties or opt for contemporary adaptations with unique accompaniments and sauces. While veal Schnitzel is a classic, pork Schnitzel, known as "Schnitzel Wiener Art," is a popular alternative and typically the more inexpensive option.

Schnitzel is frequently served with numerous side dishes, with the most common being potato salad, french fries, or a side of mixed greens. The tanginess of the potato salad or the freshness of the greens wonderfully matches the richness of the fried cutlet. Additionally, a slice of lemon is generally offered alongside the Schnitzel, allowing diners to add a zesty touch to the dish, boosting the entire flavor profile.

To enjoy the actual flavor of Schnitzel in Berlin, consider visiting some of the city's famed restaurants, taverns, or street food carts. These places generally pride themselves on employing locally sourced, high-quality foods and time-honored recipes that have been passed down through generations.

As a word of advice, bear in mind that Schnitzel quantities in Berlin can be rather big, making it a perfect dish to share with friends or family. Don't hesitate to mix it with a cool German beer or a glass of locally-produced wine for a genuinely authentic experience.

Kartoffelsalat

Kartoffelsalat, or potato salad, is characterized by its simplicity and regional variances. The essential ingredients include cooked potatoes, onions, and a dressing made from vegetable broth, vinegar, oil, and mustard. Some versions may incorporate bacon, pickles, or fresh herbs, providing a unique touch to the dish. It is commonly served warm or at room temperature, giving it an adaptable option for numerous situations.

One of the important elements of Kartoffelsalat is its historical relevance in German cuisine. Its roots may be traced back to the 18th century, and it has evolved over time to become a treasured classic. Many families in Berlin have their own cherished recipes, passed down through generations, contributing to the diversity of flavors found around the city.

Tourists in Berlin can find several options to enjoy Kartoffelsalat. Traditional German restaurants, such as "Gaststätten" or "Wirtshaus," commonly feature this meal on their menus. Additionally, food markets, especially during festive seasons like Christmas or local festivities, provide many variants of Kartoffelsalat created with passion and authenticity.

Beyond its taste and history, Kartoffelsalat symbolizes the spirit of Berlin's culinary culture. The city prides itself on its emphasis on locally-sourced and fresh ingredients. Kartoffelsalat showcases the significance of potatoes in German cuisine, a staple crop that has sustained the nation for ages.

The experience of indulging in kartoffelsalat goes beyond the food itself. It's about embracing the community nature of dining in Berlin. Whether enjoyed at a family gathering, a casual picnic in one of Berlin's lovely parks, or in the boisterous ambiance of a beer garden, Kartoffelsalat is a food that draws people together.

For tourists looking to take a bit of Kartoffelsalat's Berlin experience home with them, several local markets and specialty food stores provide pre-made or packed versions of the salad. These might be beautiful souvenirs or a great snack for the ride back.

Labskaus

Labskaus is a meal with a marine history, profoundly established in the seafaring culture of Northern Germany, particularly in ports like Hamburg and Bremen. Its name is supposed to have derived from the English term "lobscouse," a sailor's meal that presumably made its way to Germany through commerce and marine relations. Over time, it evolved and became Labskaus, a regional specialty.

The major ingredients of Labskaus often comprise corned beef, onions, potatoes, and beets. These ingredients are chopped or mashed together to create a visually spectacular blend of hues — pink from the beetroot and white from the potatoes. Some varieties may contain extra components like pickles, fried eggs, or herring on the side, improving the dish's complexity and flavor.

Preparing Labskaus is an art in itself, since each chef may have their personal take on the dish. However, the core remains the same — a substantial and fulfilling supper that was once a mainstay for sailors on lengthy travels at sea.

In Berlin, Labskaus is not as ubiquitous as in its Northern German counterparts, but numerous classic taverns and cafés cater to travelers wanting an authentic experience. One can discover Labskaus in classic German pubs and maritime-themed restaurants that celebrate the city's historical connections with the waterways.

To really appreciate Labskaus, it is vital to comprehend its history and cultural significance. A dish that fed countless sailors and mariners, it depicts the resilience and resourcefulness of people who sailed the oceans.

For the uninitiated, the flavor of Labskaus may be unexpected. The combination of corned beef, onions, potatoes, and beetroot makes a perfect blend of flavors. The moderate saltiness of the beef works beautifully with the natural sweetness of the beets, all balanced by the starchy potatoes. The extra accompaniments, such as pickles or herring, offer additional levels of flavor that complement the main dish.

Buletten

Buletten, also known as Frikadellen or Fleischpflanzerl in other regions of Germany, are essentially pan-fried meat patties made from a mixture of minced meat, often beef, pork, or a combination of both, mixed with breadcrumbs, onions, eggs, and a blend of other herbs and spices. The actual recipe might vary from one cook to another, with some adding a dash of mustard or Worcester sauce for an added boost of flavor. The mixture is then shaped into round or oval patties and pan-fried until they have a wonderfully crispy outside and juicy, tender interior.

The origins of Buletten may be traced back to the 18th century, and over time, this traditional meal has developed to adapt to varied regional tastes. In Berlin, Buletten is strongly established in the local culinary heritage, and you can find them in many places throughout the city. From street food vendors and traditional pubs to high-end restaurants, Buletten figure heavily on menus, offering both locals and visitors a taste of true Berliner cuisine.

One of the reasons why Buletten is so renowned is its adaptability. It can be served in many ways, making it ideal for varied preferences and events. Many businesses offer Buletten as a typical meal, complemented by sides like potato salad, sauerkraut, or mashed potatoes. Alternatively, they can be served as a full sandwich, packed in a bun with various toppings such as lettuce, tomatoes, and pickles.

For travelers, trying Buletten is an essential culinary experience when visiting Berlin. Sampling this meal provides an insight into the city's culture, establishing a connection to its past and the everyday life of its citizens. Moreover, Buletten is generally economical, making them an accessible and pleasant alternative for those experiencing Berlin on a budget. When searching for Buletten in Berlin, you'll likely discover several varieties of the dish due to the unique culinary landscape of the city.

Spätzle

Spätzle, commonly described as German egg noodles, are produced from simple ingredients: eggs, flour, salt, and a splash of water or milk. The word "Spätzle" stems from the Swabian dialect, where "Spätz" means "little sparrows," referring to the shape of the noodles, which can resemble small, irregularly shaped drops or elongated dumplings.

In Berlin, you can find Spätzle cooked in many ways, representing the city's rich culinary scene. The most traditional preparation involves cooking the dough until it rises to the surface, marking its readiness to be served. This results in soft, supple noodles that can be served as a side dish or as a hearty main course.

One popular version of Spätzle is to mix them with grated cheese, creating "Käsespätzle," a classic German comfort dish. The noodles are piled with substantial amounts of cheese and sometimes topped with crunchy fried onions, making it a rich and savory pleasure. Käsespätzle is popular among locals, and you can get it in many classic German cafes and beer gardens across Berlin.

Another common method to have Spätzle is with roasted meats, such as "Rahmschwammerl." This meal blends Spätzle with a creamy mushroom sauce, often accompanied by luscious slices of pig or beef. The earthy aromas of the mushrooms complement the noodles nicely, making it a must-try for those seeking a more rustic dining experience in Berlin.

Spätzle is not just about its taste but also about the pleasure of experiencing a classic German delicacy. It is often served in a pleasant, rustic ambiance, giving a warm and friendly atmosphere for guests to taste the food.

From high-end restaurants to modest family-run diners, there are lots of venues to sample delicious Spätzle. Whether you're wanting a taste of real German cuisine or simply looking for a great and substantial lunch, Spätzle is a fantastic pick that won't disappoint.

Flammkuchen

Flammkuchen, also known as tarte flambée, is a wonderful culinary pleasure that originated in the Alsace region of France but has also grown popular in Berlin. At first look, Flammkuchen may resemble a pizza due to its thin, crunchy crust, but its unique flavor profile sets it apart. The basis consists of unleavened dough, rolled out to reach a thin and crispy consistency, making it a good option for people seeking a lighter alternative to heavy dough-based dishes.

The typical Flammkuchen comes with a topping of crème fraîche, which offers a thick and creamy base to the dish. It is then lavishly covered with thinly sliced onions, which caramelize while baking, giving the dish a sweet and savory flavor. Smoked bacon or lardons are another typical addition, producing a wonderful smokiness that complements the other components.

For those wanting a vegetarian option, Flammkuchen can be served with numerous toppings like fresh mushrooms, cherry tomatoes, or even pieces of apple, which add a burst of natural sweetness. Additionally, cheese is sometimes sprinkled over the top, adding a delicious gooeyness to each bite.

The Flammkuchen is then baked in a wood-fired oven or a high-temperature conventional oven, letting the crust crisp up as the flavors melt together to create a harmonic taste experience. The outcome is a great combination of flavors, with the creamy crème fraîche, sweet caramelized onions, smokey bacon, and any other toppings melding together in each mouthful.

In Berlin, one may find Flammkuchen in many restaurants, cafés, and food markets across the city. It has been a popular choice among locals and visitors alike because of its simplicity, unusual taste, and versatility.

Flammkuchen is best served as a shared dish with friends or family, accompanied by a refreshing beverage such as a local German beer or a glass of wine, which further enriches the eating experience.

Sauerbraten

Sauerbraten traces its roots back to the medieval era and has changed over the ages. The dish often comprises delicate beef, marinated in a mixture of vinegar or wine along with a variety of aromatic spices and herbs. The marination process can continue anywhere from a few days to a week, providing a particular acidic flavor to the meat. This extended marination not only fills the beef with rich tastes but also tenderizes it, making it luscious and melt-in-your-mouth delectable.

The basic ingredients of Sauerbraten include beef (typically from the shoulder or rump), red wine or vinegar, water, onions, carrots, cloves, bay leaves, and peppercorns. The marinated beef is slow-cooked to perfection, allowing the flavors to mix and develop. The traditional recipe is frequently served with a big serving of potato dumplings (Kartoffelklöße) or boiled potatoes and red cabbage (Rotkohl), providing a beautiful balance of flavors and textures.

The word "Sauerbraten" translates to "sour roast," and as the name suggests, the meal has a wonderful tanginess that distinguishes it from other German beef dishes. The acidity from the vinegar or wine marinade is well offset by the sweetness of the red cabbage and the heartiness of the potatoes. The meat's softness and the rich, flavorful sauce make every bite a delightful experience.

Sauerbraten is not merely a dish; it's a cultural icon of German food. It symbolizes the Germans' appreciation for hearty and tasty meals that bring friends and family together. In Berlin, a city profoundly anchored in history and customs, Sauerbraten occupies a special place as a dish that bridges the gap between the past and the present, exhibiting the nation's culinary legacy.

Tourists can find Sauerbraten in several classic German restaurants, known as "Gasthäuser" or "Gaststätten," across Berlin. Some of the greatest venues to appreciate this delightful dish are ancient taverns in the city center, family-run diners in attractive districts, and even some fine dining restaurants that put a contemporary touch on this classic cuisine. Pair your dinner with a German beer or a glass of wine to compliment the flavors fully.

Conclusion
Berlin offers a pleasant culinary trip for those looking to explore the city through its different cuisines. From famous German foods like Currywurst and Schnitzel to cosmopolitan pleasures like Doner Kebabs and Falafel, there's something for every pallet. Don't forget to quench your sweet desires

with delicacies like Apfelstrudel and Berliner Pfannkuchen while enjoying the city's colorful café culture. So, be prepared to come hungry and depart with a heart full of wonderful memories and a satiated appetite.

Best Time To Visit

The best time to visit Berlin depends on individual preferences and interests, as each season provides distinct experiences and activities.

Spring (March through May)
Spring is a beautiful season to visit Berlin, as the city comes alive with flowering flowers and warm temperatures. The usual daytime temperatures vary from 10°C to 15°C, making it pleasant for outdoor explorations. The city's parks and gardens, like the famous Tiergarten and Charlottenburg Palace Gardens, are in full bloom, producing magnificent vistas suited for leisurely walks and picnics.

Additionally, Berlin hosts several outdoor events and festivals during spring, appealing to varied preferences. Visitors can enjoy cultural festivals like the Berliner Festspiele or the Carnival of Cultures, which display the city's eclectic and artistic side. Moreover, spring heralds the start of the open-air market season, with flea markets and food markets cropping up over the city, allowing an opportunity to sample local foods and shop for unique souvenirs.

Summer (June to August)
Summer is a popular tourist season in Berlin and for good reason. With temperatures ranging from 20°C to 25°C, it's the best time for sightseeing and enjoying outdoor activities. The city holds several music festivals, open-air concerts, and outdoor cinema screenings, adding to the lively atmosphere.

Visitors can indulge in Berlin's growing street food scene, relax at the city's urban beaches along the Spree River, or rent a bike to explore the city's wide network of cycling lanes. The famed Museum Island and iconic landmarks like the Brandenburg Gate and Berlin Wall Memorial are best experienced under the clear sky and extended daytime hours. However, expect greater crowds and increased accommodation fees throughout this season.

Autumn (September to November)
Autumn in Berlin brings colder temperatures, ranging from 10°C to 15°C, while the city's greenery takes on magnificent golden colors. The visitor crowds thin out compared to summer, giving for a more quiet experience. Autumn is a wonderful time for cultural fans, as the city's renowned theaters, galleries, and opera houses open their new seasons, presenting a profusion of events and exhibitions.

One of the highlights of autumn in Berlin is the Festival of Lights, during which renowned buildings and monuments are lit with stunning light displays. Moreover, wine aficionados can enjoy the Berlin Wine Festival, where vineyards from all over Germany gather to present their best vintages.

Winter (December through February)
Winter in Berlin might be frigid, with temperatures averaging around 0°C to 5°C, but it offers a unique and enchanting experience for travelers. The city turns into a winter wonderland with attractive Christmas markets sprinkled throughout, offering seasonal delicacies, crafts, and festive activities.

The historic Potsdamer Platz and the Gendarmenmarkt are some of the greatest spots to experience the stunning Christmas markets. Moreover, visiting Berlin during winter allows travelers to skip the peak tourist season, meaning shorter waits at attractions and more reasonable hotel alternatives.

Winter sports fans can enjoy ice skating at numerous rinks across the city, including the famous one at Alexanderplatz. Additionally, Berlin's cultural sector stays vibrant during winter, with theater performances, concerts, and art exhibitions.

Conclusion
Spring and summer are perfect for outdoor activities and festivals, while autumn offers a more quiet experience with cultural highlights. Winter gives a lovely Christmas mood and fewer crowds. Ultimately, no matter when you visit, Berlin's rich history, vibrant culture, and numerous attractions are likely to leave a lasting impact on every tourist.

Traveling Itinerary

A one-week holiday in Berlin offers an exciting voyage through time, from the ruins of the past to the busy metropolis of the present.

Day 1: Arrival and Introduction to Berlin
Upon arrival in Berlin, relax in your accommodation and take some time to recuperate after the travel. In the evening, walk to Alexanderplatz, a famous area teeming with bustle. Marvel at the TV Tower, a symbol of the city's reunification, and get a bird's-eye perspective from its observation deck. Nearby, visit the old Nikolaiviertel quarter and enjoy a lovely dinner at one of its quaint eateries.

Day 2: Exploring Historic Berlin
Start the day with a visit to the Berlin Wall Memorial, where you can learn about the city's partition and reunification. Then, proceed on to the Reichstag Building, the seat of the German Parliament, and ascend to its glass dome for panoramic views. Continue to Brandenburg Gate, a symbol of unification and one of Berlin's most renowned sites. Walk down Unter den Linden, a beautiful street packed with stores and old buildings.

Day 3: Museums and Art Galleries
Dedicate the third day to Berlin's world-class museums. Begin at Museum Island, a UNESCO World Heritage site, including notable institutions like the Pergamon Museum and the Neues Museum. After lunch, see the East Side Gallery, a portion of the Berlin Wall adorned in bright murals. Later, explore the Hamburger Bahnhof Museum of Contemporary Art, displaying modern treasures.

Day 4: Potsdam Day Trip
Take a day trip to Potsdam, a lovely city located just outside Berlin. Explore the beautiful Sanssouci Palace and its gorgeous grounds, a former residence of Prussian kings. Discover the Dutch Quarter with its quaint architecture, and wander along the shores of the magnificent Wannsee Lake.

Day 5: Modern Berlin
Shift gears to contemporary Berlin. Head to the fashionable neighborhood of Kreuzberg noted for its bright street art, cosmopolitan ambiance, and contemporary eateries. Visit East Side Park and enjoy the riverbank landscape. In the evening, experience Berlin's nightlife by visiting one of the city's famed clubs or enjoying live music performances.

Day 6: Charlottenburg Palace and Shopping
Explore the sumptuous Charlottenburg Palace, a spectacular specimen of baroque architecture. Take a leisurely walk through its grounds and learn about the history of Prussian royalty. Afterward, indulge in some shopping at Kurfürstendamm, one of Berlin's most famous shopping districts, offering a mix of designer boutiques and department stores.

Day 7: Tiergarten and Farewell
Spend your final day unwinding in Tiergarten, Berlin's large central park. Rent a bike or have a nice picnic amidst nature. Later, explore the adjacent Gemäldegalerie, home to a remarkable collection of European art.

In the evening, bid farewell to Berlin by enjoying a magnificent boat tour along the River Spree. As the sun sets over the city, reflect on the great experiences and memories you've accumulated during your week-long vacation.

Conclusion
This itinerary delivers a complete flavor of the city's spirit, but remember that Berlin has so much more to offer, and each visitor's experience is uniquely their own. Embrace the diversity, immerse yourself in the culture, and savor every second of your Berlin adventure.

Visiting On a Budget

While it provides a myriad of attractions, it's also easy to visit Berlin on a budget without compromising on enjoying its particular character. From modest hotels and budget-friendly activities to inexpensive dining options, here's how to visit Berlin on a budget.

Housing
Berlin features a choice of affordable housing alternatives, including hostels, guesthouses, and budget hotels. Hostels are a fantastic choice for backpackers and budget travelers, offering economical dormitory-style accommodations and public facilities to meet fellow travelers. Booking in advance and opting for shared rooms might save on costs. Additionally, Airbnb and vacation rentals may offer present more cheap possibilities, especially for small groups or longer stays.

Transit
Berlin features an efficient public transit system, which is both cost-effective and convenient. The city's vast network of buses, trams, and trains connects all main tourist destinations. Tourists can acquire a Berlin Welcome Card, which permits unlimited travel inside the city's zones and offers discounts on numerous attractions. Alternatively, renting a bike is an eco-friendly and cheap way to explore Berlin, with bike-sharing schemes accessible across the city.

Free and Budget-Friendly Attractions
Berlin's history is profoundly connected with the events of the 20th century, and numerous historical landmarks can be visited free of charge. The Brandenburg Gate, Berlin Wall

Memorial, East Side Gallery, and the Holocaust Memorial are some of the prominent attractions accessible to budget travelers. Additionally, the city is home to various parks, like Tiergarten and Mauerpark, where visitors may take leisurely strolls and even attend free open-air activities.

Museums and Galleries
While some of Berlin's renowned museums and galleries have entry prices, there are other options for budget-conscious travelers. Many institutions offer free admittance on certain days or during specific hours. The Pergamon Museum, for instance, gives free admission every first Thursday of the month. The Berlin Wall Museum and the German Historical Museum both provide unique insights into the city's past without any entry price.

Street Art and Architecture
Berlin's thriving street art scene and beautiful architecture may be experienced without spending a dime. The city is a canvas for street painters, and taking a self-guided walking tour of the bright street art in neighborhoods like Kreuzberg and Friedrichshain is a budget-friendly way to explore the city's creative energy. Additionally, Berlin's prominent architectural icons, such as the Reichstag building and the TV Tower at Alexanderplatz, offer excellent vistas and photo opportunities without any price.

Food and Dining
Exploring Berlin's street food markets and food trucks can be a cheap and entertaining way to experience new cuisines. Currywurst, a popular local fast food delicacy, is inexpensive and a must-try for visitors. Exploring neighborhoods like Neukölln and Prenzlauer Berg might lead to discovering

budget-friendly cafés and cafes that serve tasty meals at cheap prices.

Nightlife
Berlin is recognized for its bustling nightlife, and while some clubs and bars can be expensive, there are plenty of affordable options. Many bars provide happy hour specials, giving beverages at discounted pricing. Additionally, alternative and subterranean clubs frequently offer reduced entrance fees and can provide an authentic Berlin nightlife experience.

Conclusion
Visiting Berlin on a budget is entirely achievable with careful planning and wise choices. Affordable housing, utilizing public transportation, visiting free sites, and indulging in budget-friendly food options can enable travelers to experience the city's unique culture, history, and nightlife without breaking the bank. Embracing Berlin's bustling street life, creative culture, and rich history on a budget will definitely produce great experiences for any traveler.

Getting Around

Getting around this big metropolis is reasonably straightforward thanks to its fast and well-connected transit infrastructure. To make the most of your stay, it's vital to educate yourself with the various forms of transportation accessible and their individual highlights.

Public Transportation: Berlin features an extensive and reliable public transportation network that includes buses, trams, and the U-Bahn (subway) and S-Bahn (urban rail) systems. The BVG (Berliner Verkehrsbetriebe) operates these services, and a single ticket is valid for all modes within a defined pricing zone and time limit. Tickets can be purchased at ticket machines, stations, or through the BVG mobile app. The latter is especially valuable as it provides real-time information about timetables, delays, and alternate routes.

U-Bahn (Subway) and S-Bahn (Urban Rail): The U-Bahn covers most locations within the city, connecting important tourist attractions and neighborhoods. The S-Bahn, on the other hand, reaches the outskirts of Berlin and is useful for reaching sites like Potsdam or Schönefeld Airport. Both networks are recognized for their timeliness and frequency, with trains coming every few minutes during peak hours.

Buses and Trams: Buses and trams complement the U-Bahn and S-Bahn services, reaching portions of the city not covered by the train network. While trams are a scenic choice, buses offer more flexibility. Both are good choices for exploring neighborhoods and uncovering lesser-known gems.

Cycling: Berlin is a bike-friendly city with an extensive network of bike lanes and pathways. Renting a bike is a popular and eco-friendly method to move around, especially in the warmer months. Numerous bike rental businesses and stations are accessible throughout the city. Keep in mind that Berlin is very flat, making cycling an attractive and accessible choice for travelers.

Taxis & Ride-Sharing: Taxis are frequently available and clearly distinguishable by their beige color and lit rooftop sign. Ride-sharing businesses like Uber are also functioning in Berlin. While more expensive than public transit, they can be useful, especially during late-night hours or when you're rushed for time.

Walking: Berlin is a city best visited on foot, particularly in the central sections. Walking allows you to immerse yourself in the city's ambiance, stumble upon hidden jewels, and appreciate its gorgeous architecture and street art.

Tourist Passes: Consider obtaining a Berlin Welcome Card (www.berlin-welcomecard.de/en), a pass that offers unrestricted travel on public transit within defined zones for a chosen term (e.g., 48 hours, 72 hours). It also provides discounts on many attractions, restaurants, and shopping. The card can save both time and money for individuals planning to visit many places.

Accessibility: Berlin's public transit system is relatively accessible for individuals with reduced mobility, with most stations having elevators and escalators. Low-floor buses and specific spots for wheelchairs are also available. The BVG provides thorough information about accessible routes and services on its website.

Remember that Berlin's transit system operates on an honor system, so verify you have a valid ticket before boarding and have it with you throughout your ride. Ticket inspectors occasionally check for legitimate tickets, and fines for fare evasion can be considerable.

Conclusion
Getting around Berlin is a snap due to its excellent public transportation, bike choices, and walkability. With careful planning and a tourist pass in hand, you can make the most of your time visiting this bustling and historic city, ensuring an outstanding trip full of cultural discoveries and memorable sites.

Shopping for Souvenirs

For any traveler visiting this enchanting city, buying souvenirs is an essential part of the adventure, from traditional German crafts to contemporary designs, Berlin provides an array of unique mementos that embody its rich history and cultural diversity. Here are the top places to shop for souvenirs in Berlin, the types of souvenirs available, and advice for a wonderful shopping experience.

Best Places for Souvenir Shopping

Alexanderplatz: Located in the middle of the city, Alexanderplatz is a bustling shopping zone boasting several shops and stores that appeal to travelers looking for gifts. The World Clock and TV Tower are prominent monuments that serve as excellent meeting spots. Shops near this location provide an assortment of gifts, including postcards, keychains, and magnets.

Kurfürstendamm (Ku'damm): One of the most famous shopping streets in Berlin, Ku'damm is lined with high-end boutiques, department stores, and souvenir shops. Here, you'll find a vast assortment of souvenirs, ranging from luxury things to modest trinkets, allowing travelers to find something to fit any budget.

Hackescher Markt: This trendy district boasts a strong arts scene and is home to diverse boutiques and craft shops. Visitors can browse through an array of handmade gifts, such as classic German ceramics, beautiful prints, and unusual clothing items.

Prenzlauer Berg: This lovely region is a haven for boutique shopping. It provides a combination of vintage shops, independent boutiques, and artisanal stores, making it a perfect destination for people seeking unique and authentic souvenirs.

Boxhagener Platz Flea Market: Held every Sunday, the Boxhagener Platz Flea Market is a delight for bargain hunters and collectors alike. Visitors can unearth vintage artifacts, antiques, and one-of-a-kind souvenirs while immersing themselves in the bustling ambiance.

Types of Souvenirs

Ampelmännchen Merchandise: The Ampelmännchen, the iconic pedestrian traffic signal figure from former East Germany, has become a symbol of Berlin's reunification. Souvenir stores provide numerous Ampelmännchen-themed goods, including mugs, T-shirts, and tote bags.

Berlin Wall Memorabilia: Pieces of the Berlin Wall, covered with vibrant graffiti, have been conserved and converted into unique mementos. Tourists can purchase bits of the wall, artworks, and postcards as physical souvenirs of this historic monument.

Beer Steins and Glasses: Germany is famed for its beer culture, and purchasing classic beer steins or glasses depicting Berlin motifs is a popular souvenir choice among tourists.

Traditional German Crafts: Berlin's markets and craft shops offer an array of traditional German crafts, such as wooden toys, handcrafted ornaments, and beautifully carved cuckoo clocks.

Currywurst Ketchup: Currywurst is incomplete without its characteristic ketchup. Jars of this delightful sauce make for a pleasant and useful memento option.

Berlin-themed Apparel: Tourists may purchase a wide choice of clothing items with Berlin-inspired designs, including T-shirts, sweatshirts, and hats, to express their love for the city elegantly.

Shopping Tips for an Enjoyable Experience

Cash vs. Card: While most establishments take credit cards, bringing some cash is advisable, especially when shopping at flea markets or smaller vendors.

Tax-Free Shopping: Non-EU travelers are eligible for tax rebates on purchases above a specified value. Look for the "Tax-Free Shopping" emblem and follow the proper procedures to receive your refund at the airport before departing.

Bargaining: Bargaining is not a typical practice in ordinary stores, but at flea markets, you may attempt negotiating for a cheaper price, especially if buying many goods.

Shop Opening Hours: In Germany, many shops close early on Saturdays and remain closed on Sundays. Plan your purchasing properly to avoid disappointment.

Quality over Quantity: While it's tempting to acquire multiple mementos, consider quality over quantity. Invest in things that genuinely reflect Berlin's culture and craftsmanship.

Conclusion

Souvenir shopping in Berlin is an exciting excursion that allows travelers to bring a bit of the city's colorful culture and history back home with them. From renowned Ampelmännchen goods to parts of the Berlin Wall, the city provides a broad assortment of souvenirs that cater to all tastes and budgets. By discovering the greatest shopping locations and adhering to some important guidelines, travelers may ensure a memorable and delightful shopping experience in this enchanting metropolis. So, next time you find yourself in Berlin, immerse yourself in its unique souvenirs and take home a part of its exceptional charm.

Tour Package Options

Berlin provides a choice of tour package options geared to meet every traveler's preferences and interests. Whether you're a history buff, an art enthusiast, a foodie, or just looking to immerse yourself in a dynamic metropolitan atmosphere, Berlin has it all. Here are the many tour package options offered to travelers in Berlin.

Historical Tours
For history buffs, Berlin is a treasure mine of renowned landmarks and heartbreaking locations that reflect the city's stormy past. Historical trips often include visits to the Berlin Wall Memorial, Brandenburg Gate, Reichstag Building, and Checkpoint Charlie. Guided by qualified historians, these tours delve deep into Berlin's vital role throughout World War II, the Cold War, and its reunification, allowing tourists to appreciate the significance of these historical events.

Cultural and Art Tours
Berlin is recognized for its strong arts and entertainment scene. Art fans can select tours that display the city's outstanding assortment of museums, galleries, and street art. The Museum Island, a UNESCO World Heritage site, is home to the Pergamon Museum and the Altes Museum, housing large art collections from various centuries. Additionally, street art excursions in places like Kreuzberg and Friedrichshain provide insight into Berlin's flourishing urban art culture.

Culinary Tours
Foodies will enjoy Berlin's numerous gastronomic choices. Food tours take travelers on a gourmet adventure through bustling food markets, fashionable cafes, and traditional

German restaurants. Sample currywurst, döner kebabs, and artisanal brews, while learning about Berlin's culinary history and the influences that have molded its food.

Nightlife and Entertainment Tours
As the sun sets, Berlin changes into a nightlife hub with an electric atmosphere. Nightlife tours cater to party-goers, guiding them around the city's biggest clubs, bars, and music venues. Berlin's techno culture is legendary, and tours often include visits to world-renowned techno clubs like Berghain and Watergate.

Day Trips and Excursions
For those seeking a larger experience beyond the city limits, day trips and excursions are appropriate. Visit the historic city of Potsdam, home to the gorgeous Sanssouci Palace and beautiful gardens. Explore the Sachsenhausen Concentration Camp Memorial, presenting a somber reflection on the crimes of the Holocaust. Nature aficionados can embark on treks to neighboring forests, lakes, and countryside for a calm vacation.

Shopping Tours
Berlin is a shopper's paradise, with a wealth of shopping opportunities to suit every taste and budget. Shopping trips encompass prominent shopping districts like Kurfürstendamm, Friedrichstrasse, and Hackescher Markt. From upscale boutiques to vintage stores and flea markets, buyers can find unique gifts and stylish products.

Conclusion
Berlin offers a rich tapestry of tour package alternatives, offering a full and fascinating experience for every traveler. Whether you're interested in history, culture, art, gastronomy,

nightlife, or shopping, Berlin caters to all inclinations. Engaging with knowledgeable guides and passionate residents adds dimension to your tour, helping you to connect with the city in a more intimate way.

Before choosing a tour package, consider your interests, time available, and money. Research reliable tour operators and read reviews from prior visitors to ensure a high-quality experience. Regardless of the tour package you choose, Berlin's charm, history, and contemporary attractiveness are guaranteed to leave an everlasting imprint on your heart and mind.

Tourist Safety Tips

While it promises a wonderful experience, protecting your safety during your visit is of utmost significance. Here are tourist safety recommendations to help you explore the city comfortably and have a worry-free journey.

Stay Informed and Plan Ahead
Before beginning your Berlin excursion, gather as much information as possible regarding the city's safety features. Research the neighborhoods you wish to visit, the local customs, emergency numbers, and healthcare facilities. Additionally, develop a basic itinerary listing the sites you desire to investigate and share it with someone trustworthy back home.

Choose Accommodations Wisely
Opt for rooms in reliable neighborhoods known for their safety and proximity to main attractions. Look for reviews from past visitors to ensure a great experience. When booking, select hotels with security measures like surveillance cameras, key card access, and 24/7 staff availability.

Use Reliable Transportation
Berlin boasts an efficient public transit system. Utilize official services like buses, trams, and the subway to navigate around the city. Be cautious when using cabs, ensuring they are licensed and have a properly visible identity. Avoid unregistered or unofficial vehicles to prevent potential scams.

Mind Your Belongings
As in every major metropolis, petty theft can occur. Keep your belongings secure at all times, especially in busy settings like

public transport. Use a cross-body bag and avoid showing pricey stuff like jewelry and devices openly. Be careful of pickpockets, particularly in tourist-heavy areas.

Respect Local Laws and Customs
Understanding and respecting Berlin's local rules and customs will help you avoid unneeded difficulties. For example, jaywalking is forbidden, and smoking is restricted in specific public locations. Familiarize yourself with the do's and don'ts to guarantee a smooth and respectful encounter with locals and authorities.

Be Cautious with Strangers
While Berlin is typically a secure city, exercise caution when dealing with strangers, especially in nightlife areas. Avoid accepting drinks from someone you don't know well, and be wary of over-friendly folks. Stick to well-populated locations and go with a partner if feasible, particularly at night.

Emergency Contact Information
Program critical emergency numbers, like local police, ambulance services, and your country's embassy, into your phone. In case of any sad situation, you will have fast access to the necessary aid.

Be Aware of Scams
Tourist spots might attract scam artists who prey on naive visitors. Beware of individuals trying to offer false tickets, overpriced souvenirs, or deceptive tour packages. Always purchase tickets from approved suppliers and verify tour operators' credentials before booking.

Watch Out for Cyclists

Berlin is a bicycle-friendly city with numerous cyclists on the road. Stay careful when crossing intersections and pay attention to bike lanes. Look both ways before crossing, and never assume a cyclist will stop for pedestrians.

Stay Hydrated and Mind the Weather
During the summer, Berlin may get pretty warm, so carry a water bottle and remain hydrated. Also, prepare adequate attire for the weather conditions during your visit, as surprise rain showers are not uncommon.

Conclusion
Berlin provides a unique blend of history, culture, and entertainment, making it an intriguing destination for travelers worldwide. By following these detailed safety precautions, you may optimize your fun while reducing any risks. Keep yourself informed, prepare ahead, and be attentive to your surroundings to guarantee a memorable and secure vacation in this enchanting city.

Festival and Events

Throughout the year, Berlin hosts a diversity of festivities, fairs, and meetings that appeal to a wide range of interests, drawing people from all corners of the globe. From historical commemorations to current music festivals, Berlin's event calendar is an intrinsic element of its character and attractiveness.

One of the most renowned events in Berlin is the Berlin International Film Festival, often known as the Berlinale, held annually in February. As one of the world's leading film festivals, it attracts filmmakers, actors, and cinephiles from around the world. The festival features a broad range of international films, from thought-provoking dramas to avant-garde pieces, and offers an opportunity for guests to enjoy the splendor of the silver screen.

Another important event is the Berlin Fashion Week, held twice a year in January and July. It is a bright spectacle where fashion designers, models, and industry insiders converge to display the latest trends and designs. The event features runway displays, exhibitions, and parties, providing a unique view into the world of fashion and style.

The Lollapalooza Berlin event, generally held in September, is an unforgettable experience. This two-day music festival boasts an incredible lineup of worldwide and local musicians across many genres, from rock and pop to electronic and hip-hop. Lollapalooza gathers a varied crowd, generating an electrifying environment within the renowned Tempelhof Airport site.

As the summer sun bathes the city in warmth, the Carnival of Cultures takes center stage in June. Celebrating Berlin's cosmopolitan identity, this celebration promotes variety via vivid parades, music, dancing, and food from around the world. Visitors can immerse themselves in the kaleidoscope of colors and feel the city's inclusive atmosphere.

The historical significance of Berlin is not neglected, and events like the Berlin Wall Anniversary on November 9th mark the collapse of the Berlin Wall in 1989. The community comes together to remember this critical event in history, with exhibitions, performances, and memorial ceremonies. Tourists can witness how this tragedy shaped the city and the lives of its citizens.

For admirers of contemporary art, the Gallery Weekend Berlin in April provides a unique opportunity to experience the city's burgeoning art scene. Hundreds of galleries open their doors to present works by both young and known artists, making it an art lover's heaven.

In December, Berlin transforms into a wintry paradise with its stunning Christmas markets. These festive marketplaces are distributed around the city, with the Gendarmenmarkt Christmas Market being one of the most prominent. Tourists can indulge in exquisite seasonal delights, and enjoy traditional music and entertainment.

Berlin also offers countless more festivals and events that cater to varied interests and niches. Whether it's the Berlin Marathon for sports fans, the Long Night of Museums for culture junkies, or the Berlinale Street Food Market for foodies, there is something for everyone.

Conclusion

Berlin's festivals and events give travelers an enriching and multifaceted experience. From the glitz and glamour of the film festival to the celebration of cultural variety, and from the throbbing beats of music festivals to the contemplation of historical moments, each event contributes to the city's vibrant and unique character. Visitors to Berlin are sure to find something that resonates with their interests and passions, making their journey to the German city an unforgettable one.

Printed in Great Britain
by Amazon